LEADERSHIP

BECOMING A DISCIPLE

Becoming Small Group
Leaders

SERENDIPITY
HOUSE

GROUP DIRECTORY

Pass this Directory around and have your Group Members
fill in their names and phone numbers

Name   Phone

_____   _____

_____   _____

_____   _____

_____   _____

_____   _____

_____   _____

_____   _____

_____   _____

_____   _____

_____   _____

_____   _____

_____   _____

_____   _____

_____   _____

_____   _____

BECOMING A DISCIPLE

Becoming Small Group Leaders

EDITING AND PRODUCTION TEAM:

Keith Madsen, Lyman Coleman, James F. Couch, Jr.,
Mary Chatfield, Ashley Benedict, Scott Lee

SERENDIPITY
HOUSE

NASHVILLE, TENNESSEE

Published by Serendipity House Publishers
Nashville, Tennessee

International Standard Book Number: 1-57494-099-6

ACKNOWLEDGMENTS

Scripture quotations are taken from the Holman Christian Standard Bible,
© Copyright 2000 by Holman Bible Publishers. Used by permission.

03 04 05 06 07 08 / 10 9 8 7 6 5 4 3 2 1

Nashville, Tennessee
1-800-525-9563
www.serendipityhouse.com

TABLE OF CONTENTS

CORE VALUES

Community: The purpose of this curriculum is to build community within the body of believers around Jesus Christ.

Group Process: To build community, the curriculum must be designed to take a group through a step-by-step process of sharing your story with one another.

Interactive Bible Study: To share your "story," the approach to Scripture in the curriculum needs to be open-ended and right brain—to "level the playing field" and encourage everyone to share.

Developmental Stages: To provide a healthy program throughout the four stages of the life cycle of a group, the curriculum needs to offer courses on three levels of commitment: (1) Beginner Level—low-level entry, high structure, to level the playing field; (2) Growth Level—deeper Bible study, flexible structure, to encourage group accountability; (3) Discipleship Level—in-depth Bible study, open structure, to move the group into high gear.

Target Audiences: To build community throughout the culture of the church, the curriculum needs to be flexible, adaptable and transferable into the structure of the average church.

Mission: To expand the kingdom of God one person at a time by filling the "empty chair." (We add an extra chair to each group session to remind us of our mission.)

FELT NEED SURVEY

Rank the following factors in order of importance to you with 1 being the highest and 5 being the lowest:

_____ The passage of Scripture that is being studied.

_____ The topic or issue that is being discussed.

_____ The affinity of group members (age, vocation, interest).

_____ The mission of the group (service projects, evangelism, starting groups).

_____ Personal encouragement.

Rank the following spiritual development needs in order of interest to you with 1 being the highest and 5 being the lowest:

_____ Learning how to become a follower of Christ.

_____ Gaining a basic understanding of the truths of the faith.

_____ Improving my disciplines of devotion, prayer, reading Scripture.

_____ Gaining a better knowledge of what is in the Bible.

_____ Applying the truths of Scripture to my life.

Of the various studies below, check the appropriate circles that indicate: if you would be interested in studying for your personal needs (P), you think would be helpful for your group (G), or you have friends that are not in the group that would come to a study of this subject (F).

	P	G	F
Growing in Christ Series (7-week studies)			
Keeping Your Cool: Dealing With Stress	O	O	O
Personal Audit: Assessing Your Life	O	O	O
Seasons of Growth: Stages of Marriage	O	O	O
Checking Your Moral Compass: Personal Morals	O	O	O
Women of Faith (8 weeks)	O	O	O
Men of Faith	O	O	O
Being Single and the Spiritual Pursuit	O	O	O
Becoming a Disciple (7-week studies)			
Discovering God's Will	O	O	O
Time for a Checkup	O	O	O
Learning to Love	O	O	O
Becoming Small Group Leaders	O	O	O
Making Great Kids	O	O	O
Foundations of the Faith (7-week studies)			
Knowing Jesus	O	O	O
Foundational Truths	O	O	O
The Christian in a Postmodern World	O	O	O
God and the Journey to Truth	O	O	O
Understanding the Savior (13-week studies)			
Mark 1–8: Jesus, the Early Years	O	O	O

	P	G	F
Mark 8–16: Jesus, the Final Days	○	○	○
John 1–11: God in the Flesh	○	○	○
John 12–21: The Passion of the Son	○	○	○
The Miracles of Jesus	○	○	○
The Life of Christ	○	○	○
The Parables of Jesus	○	○	○
The Sermon on the Mount: Jesus, the Teacher	○	○	○

The Message of Paul

	P	G	F
Romans 1–7: Who We Really Are (13 weeks)	○	○	○
Romans 8–16: Being a Part of God's Plan (13 weeks)	○	○	○
1 Corinthians: Taking on Tough Issues (13 weeks)	○	○	○
Galatians: Living by Grace (13 weeks)	○	○	○
Ephesians: Together in Christ (12 weeks)	○	○	○
Philippians: Running the Race (7 weeks)	○	○	○

Words of Faith

	P	G	F
Acts 1–14: The Church on Fire (13 weeks)	○	○	○
Acts 15–28: The Irrepressible Witness (13 weeks)	○	○	○
Hebrews: Jesus Through the Eyes of Hebrew Faith (13 weeks)	○	○	○
James: Faith at Work (12 weeks)	○	○	○
1 Peter: Staying the Course (10 weeks)	○	○	○
1 John: Walking in the Light (11 weeks)	○	○	○
Revelation 1–12: End of Time (13 weeks)	○	○	○
Revelation 13–22: The New Jerusalem (13 weeks)	○	○	○

301 Bible Studies with Homework Assignments (13-week studies)

	P	G	F
Ephesians: Our Riches in Christ	○	○	○
James: Walking the Talk	○	○	○
Life of Christ: Behold the Man	○	○	○
Miracles: Signs and Wonders	○	○	○
Parables: Virtual Reality	○	○	○
Philippians: Joy Under Stress	○	○	○
Sermon on the Mount: Examining Your Life	○	○	○
1 John: The Test of Faith	○	○	○

Felt Need Series (7-week studies)

	P	G	F
Stress Management: Finding the Balance	○	○	○
12 Steps: The Path to Wholeness	○	○	○
Divorce Recovery: Picking Up the Pieces	○	○	○
Parenting Adolescents: Easing the Way to Adulthood	○	○	○
Blended Families: Yours, Mine, Ours	○	○	○
Dealing with Grief and Loss: Hope in the Midst of Pain	○	○	○
Healthy Relationships: Living Within Defined Boundaries	○	○	○
Marriage Enrichment: Making a Good Marriage Better	○	○	○

SESSION 1

Connected to the Vine

SCRIPTURE: John 15:1-17

LEADER

Make sure that each participant reads and studies this section prior to this first session. Explain to the group that this will be a unique small group. Because they are in training to be group leaders and discussion facilitators, they will be expected to read the entire session before you come together. The group will be covering only the discussion questions at each meeting. Each individual will be responsible to understand the introductory material for each session

Welcome to this training for those who are preparing to be small-group leaders. This study is based on the premise that we learn by doing. As we become a group ourselves, we will also learn what a leader can do to help a group bond together while they share their stories. This won't just be an academic exercise. We really will learn to know and care for each other, so what we experience will be valuable in its own right. But much more so than with most group studies, we will also pay attention to the processes and how we can facilitate them later in our own groups.

As with all Serendipity small-groups, the process starts with Scripture. We will look at stories in the Bible and learn what God says to us through them, as well as use them to share our own stories. The Scriptural passages of this series will all relate to important processes in group development. Specifically we will look at:

- **Connecting to Each Other by Connecting with Christ.** Like a vine holds its branches together, so Christ is what holds us together. If we want to be close as a Christian small group, we must therefore start by connecting the group to Christ. We will learn about this in Session One by looking at John 15:1-17.

- **Helping Others Tell Their Story.** Each of us has a story to tell, and we cannot be really known until our individual stories are heard. Many of us have a hard time telling our stories. Maybe its shyness, maybe it's lack of verbal ability, or maybe it's because we have been burned when we opened up. For whatever reason, many of us have a hard time being personal. A small-group leader must help the group members to risk being open. We will learn about this important process in Session Two as we consider the story of the Samaritan woman by the well in John 4:1-26.

• **Affirming Each Other**. A Christian small group is built as we encourage each other and help each other feel good about who we are and our value in the sight of God. The Apostle Paul practiced this in nearly all of his letters by affirming the people to whom he was writing. In Session Three we will look at a good example of this practice in Philippians 1:3-11.

• **Finding Our Giftedness**. We all need to know how we can contribute. What can I do to make a difference in this group, and indeed in my world? The Bible teaches us that each of us is gifted by God to benefit the common good. Being part of a group of caring people meeting together can help us discover what our gifts are, as well as learn to use and celebrate them. We will explore this part of group development in Session Four by looking at 1 Corinthians 12:7-31. We will also consider what this implies for our need for each other.

• **Giving Mutual Admonition**. This is a tough one. Webster's Dictionary defines "admonish" as "giving mild reproof to" or "to warn against." The hard part about this is that so many want to do this as the know-it-all who tells the other people around them the truth about how it is. No one likes that. That is why in Serendipity groups we make it a rule that we do not give unsolicited advice (see the covenant below). However, it is also true that sometimes, in the proper context, we need to share insights with each other, and even warn one another if we see a brother or sister heading into dangerous territory. The key here is that such admonition should be mutual. We need to receive it as well as give it. It also needs to be given when the other person has indicated an openness to it. This is how we learn and grow, because none of us has arrived yet. In looking at this potentially difficult area of group life, we will consider Acts 18:18-28 and see how the early Christians admonished one another. This will be our focus in Session Five.

• **Dealing with Controversy**. We will not all see things the same in this group, nor will people in the group that you lead. Sometimes we may even have strong feelings on the opposite side of a controversial subject. How do we deal with that? To examine this challenge we will look at how the disciples met one of the hot controversies in the early church, the matter of which Jewish traditions Gentile converts must follow. They had a church council on this subject in Jerusalem, and the decisions of this meeting are reported in Acts 15. In Session Six we will look at Acts 15:1-21 to examine this controversy and what it means for group life.

• **The Centrality of Prayer**. Prayer is a vital part of every Serendipity group. We use it to express our care for one another and to draw on the power of God in meeting the challenges of life. While you will have experienced this prayer in each of the previous six sessions, in Session Seven we will consider Acts 12:1-17 and what it says about the power of prayer.

- **Mission and Multiplication**. The goal of Christian small groups is not to become a clique that never looks beyond their group. The goal is rather to experience Christian community that can be replicated in similar groups. We always seek to start new groups and continue sharing the community experience. We will look at this aspect of groups in Session Eight by studying together Acts 8:1-8, 14-17.

As we look at these passages and share together, it is important that we do so as a caring group. Becoming such a group does not just happen — it requires that we agree together to certain ways of doing things. This necessitates that we covenant with each other. A group covenant is a "contract" that spells out our expectations and ground rules for our group. We will have such a covenant in this group, and it is expected that each of the groups you lead will also have a covenant. Such a covenant is a way of assuring each other that each member will invest themselves fully in the process and that confidentiality will be preserved. It will normally be in the front of the book prior to the first session. However, in this book for group leaders, we include it here in this first session.

GROUND RULES

- **Priority**: While you are in the group, you give the group meeting priority.

- **Participation**: Everyone participates and no one dominates.

- **Respect**: Everyone is given the right to their own opinion and all questions are encouraged and respected.

- **Confidentiality**: Anything that is said in the meeting is never repeated outside the meeting.

- **Empty Chair**: The group stays open to new people at every meeting. While this is true of our regular groups, it is not true of this particular group, since our purpose is to train leaders and candidates for group leadership need to experience the full course. Therefore, all of the group members need to be in every session and none should be added after the group begins.

- **Support**: Permission is given to call upon each other in time of need — even in the middle of the night.

- **Advice Giving**: Unsolicited advice is not allowed.

- **Mission**: We agree to do everything in our power to start a new group as our mission.

GOALS

• The time and place this group is going to meet is _____.

• Responsibility for refreshments is _____.

• Child care is _____ responsibility.

• This group will meet until _____ at which time we will decide to split into new groups or continue our sessions together. In our case, we will meet for eight sessions, and it is expected that each of us will be leaders of new groups after we have completed this course.

• Our primary purpose for meeting is: _____.

OUR SMALL GROUP COVENANT

1. The facilitator for this group is _____.

2. The apprentice facilitator for this group is _____.

3. This group will meet from _____ to _____ on _____.

4. This group will normally meet at _____.

5. Child care will be arranged by _____.

6. Refreshments will be coordinated by _____.

7. Our primary purpose for meeting is _____.

8. Our secondary purpose for meeting is _____.

We all agree to follow the ground rules listed below:

a. This meeting will be given priority in our schedules.
b. Everyone will participate in each meeting and no one will dominate a meeting.
c. Each has a right to one's own opinion and all questions will be respected.
d. Everything that is said in group meetings is never to be repeated outside of the meeting.
e. This group will be open to new people at every meeting.
f. Permission is given for all to call on each other in time of need.
g. Unsolicited advice is not allowed.
h. We agree to fill the empty chair and work toward starting new groups.

We are to hold one another accountable to meet any commitments mutually agreed upon by this group.

I agree to all of the above _____ date _____

By sharing honestly with each other in these sessions, holding to these ground rules and opening our hearts fully to God's direction, we will take some important steps in growing as leaders and helping the groups we lead to have a life-changing experience together. Let's begin our journey together!

***LEADER

In order to give each person being trained as a leader experience in leading, assign a different member of the group each week to lead the Icebreaker part of the session. In leading the Icebreaker it is important to have each person share. If your group is large, subdivide your group into groups of three to six persons. This helps all to share fully without the meeting becoming excessively long, and it also helps shy persons to share more easily. To help your group members get acquainted, introduce each person, and then take turns answering all three of the Icebreaker questions.

An important part of knowing each other is knowing our roots, our family tree. Genealogical study is quite popular today because the internet makes it so much easier and because people are curious about who went before them. Share something about what you know of your own roots by answering the following questions.

1. From what you know of your family tree, which of the following is it most like?
   - a walnut tree – chock full of nuts
   - a giant Sequoia – huge, with deep and ancient roots
   - a flowering crabapple – adding color to the world, although with some "sour fruit" as well
   - an alpine fir – weathered by the tough times
   - a vine – spread out everywhere
   - a peach tree – full of succulent fruit
   - a weeping willow – graceful, but full of sadness
   - other _____

2. Which of your grandparents or great-grandparents did you find most interesting? What did they tell you about your other ancestors?

3. How strongly connected do you feel right now to the others on your family tree?
   - Not at all – I'm like a branch the wind has blown off.
   - Just barely – I'm like a broken branch still attached by a thin strip of bark.
   - I'm just an insignificant little branch no one else notices.
   - I'm a strong branch, holding my own.
   - I'm one of the main branches holding many other branches together.
   - other _____

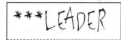

***LEADER

Select a person from the group ahead of time to read aloud the Scripture passage.

Jesus used many analogies from nature: the birds of the air, the lilies of the field, seed growing in different kinds of ground, and here a vine with many branches. Through this image of the vine Jesus sought to help his disciples see how important it was to remain connected. They couldn't thrive on their own. They needed to stay attached to Him, and through Him to the rest of the disciples, the rest of the "branches". This underlines the importance of our groups: they help us to remain connected. Staying connected to Jesus and to each other helps us to be more "fruitful" in our lives as Christians.

Read John 15:1-17, and then discuss the Questions for Interaction, dividing into sub-groups of three to six persons. Be sure to save time at the end for the Caring Time.

15 "I am the true vine, and My Father is the vineyard keeper. ² Every branch in Me that does not produce fruit He removes, and He prunes every branch that produces fruit so that it will produce more fruit. ³ You are already clean because of the word I have spoken to you. ⁴ Remain in Me, and I in you. Just as a branch is unable to produce fruit by itself unless it remains on the vine, so neither can you unless you remain in Me.

⁵ "I am the vine; you are the branches. The one who remains in Me and I in him produces much fruit, because you can do nothing without Me. ⁶ If anyone does not remain in Me, he is thrown aside like a branch and he withers. They gather them, throw them into the fire, and they are burned. ⁷ If you remain in Me and My words remain in you, ask whatever you want and it will be done for you. ⁸ My Father is glorified by this: that you produce much fruit and prove to be My disciples.

⁹ "Just as the Father has loved Me, I also have loved you. Remain in My love. ¹⁰ If you keep My commandments you will remain in My love, just as I have kept My Father's commandments and remain in His love.

¹¹ "I have spoken these things to you so that My joy may be in you and your joy may be complete. ¹² This is My commandment: that you love one another just as I have loved you. ¹³ No one has greater love than this, that someone would lay down his life for his friends. ¹⁴ You are My friends if you do what I command you. ¹⁵ I do not call you slaves anymore, because a slave doesn't know what his master is doing. I have called you friends, because I have made known to you everything I have heard from My Father. ¹⁶ You did not choose Me, but I chose you. I appointed you that you should go out and produce fruit, and that your fruit should remain, so that whatever you ask the Father in My name, He will give you. ¹⁷ This is what I command you: that you love one another.

John 15:1-17

QUESTIONS FOR INTERACTION

The opening question in this study is a lighter question relating the story to one's own personal experience. Go around and have each person share on this question in turn. Questions numbered 2 to 6 relate to understanding the content of the passage. Persons should be encouraged to respond to these questions at will. Questions numbered 7 and 8 help group members apply the text to their own personal lives, and once again on these the leader should have each person share on the question in turn.

1. What kind of gardener are you?
   - One that kills everything I touch.
   - A neglectful one – I want to put in the plant, then not bother with it.
   - A modern one – plastic plants are more my style.
   - A nurturing one – I love to help things grow.
   - One with a green thumb – plants thrive in my care.
   - other _____

2. What is the significance of the fact that the Father as our spiritual gardener "prunes" every branch of the vine?

3. In terms of the Christian life, what is meant by a branch "producing fruit"? Why is remaining connected to Christ essential to producing this fruit?

4. What are important disciplines for a person to follow in order to remain connected to the vine that is Jesus Christ? What part can a group like this play in the process?

5. How is the command repeated in verses 12 and 17 related to the idea of remaining connected to the vine?

6. How did Christ demonstrate this greatest kind of love that he wants us to show to each other?

7. How solidly are you connected to the vine of Jesus Christ right now?
   - Not at all – I'm like a branch the wind has blown off.
   - Just barely – I'm like a broken branch still attached by a thin strip of bark

- I'm just an insignificant little branch no one else notices.
- I'm a strong branch, holding my own.
- I'm one of the main branches holding many other branches together.
- other _____

8. As a group leader, how can God best use you to "strengthen the vine"?

 GOING DEEPER: *If your group has time and/or wants a challenge, go on to these questions.*

9. Jesus says "Greater love has no one than this, that he lay down his life for his friends." What is the difference between such self-sacrificing friendship and having a "martyr complex"?

10. What implications are there for group leaders in Jesus' promise, "whatever you ask the Father in My name, He will give to you"?

CARING TIME *Apply the Lesson & Pray for One another* | **15 Min.**

***LEADER

This very important time is to develop and express your concern for each other as group members by praying for one another. In this first session, the leader should pray for the requests shared by the group. First have group members respond to the following questions.

Note that we are using a progression of prayers through the various session to teach members how to pray in public. In each of the first five sessions we will model prayer first and then gradually lead them into more personal responsibility in group prayers. If this were a normal group, we would ask the group to pray for the empty chair in several of the sessions. This furthers the mission of starting new groups and bringing people into the kingdom. It would be inappropriate in this group dedicated to training new leaders to ask outsiders to join the group.

1. Pray that God will attach all of you more securely to the vine of Jesus Christ during the course of this study.

2. How can this group be in prayer for you that you feel more connected to your brothers and sisters around you?

3. What do you need to ask for in Jesus' name right now that will make you a better group leader?

NEXT WEEK

Today we began by considering the necessity of being attached to the "vine" of Jesus Christ, and what role a small group can play in that process. Next week we will see how Jesus helped the Samaritan woman at the well tell her story, and what it says to us about helping group members tell their story. We will consider the importance of listening, and we will see how hearing each other's story helps us to grow closer as a group. Make sure that you read the short Introduction section at the beginning of Session Two prior to the session.

NOTES ON JOHN 15:1-17

Summary: In John, Jesus uses a variety of "I am" statements to define who He is and what His mission is. In this chapter He defines himself as being like a vine. It would have been a natural allusion in a land where grapes were an important crop. The people would understand that a vine that didn't produce fruit wouldn't be worth much. They would also understand that in order to be most productive, a vine would have to have unproductive branches trimmed off. A branch that somehow became separated from the vine would also become useless (v.6.) This allusion was giving a message to those who were followers of Jesus. They would be facing persecution and there would be the temptation to "separate themselves from the vine." Jesus was telling them in advance that such an action would result in them being unproductive and ultimately judged by God (v.6). Only by remaining connected to Christ can a person live a productive life with the promise of eternal life to follow.

In the middle of the passage, Jesus switches to a different kind of connection image – that of friends. This is a positive companion of the more negative image of the judgment of the unproductive vine. If the disciples remain connected to Christ, they have the opportunity to consider themselves a friend of Jesus. The rewarding part of this is that Jesus is the friend par excellence. He even goes to the extent of laying down His life for his friends, the ultimate act of friendship. In this kind of friendship and love, we have an example to follow in learning what true love really is.

15:1 I am the true vine. The image of the vine was used to describe Israel in the Old Testament (Ps. 80:14-18; Isa. 5:1-7). But Israel did not produce the fruits God expected (Isa. 5:1-7; Matt. 21:43). Jesus transfers this image to Himself. He is the "true vine" who, because He always does what pleases the Father (8:29), produces fruit for God.

15:2 removes...prunes. A gardener cuts off dead branches that do not contribute to the plant, and trims small branches so that when they grow back they might be stronger. This "pruning" can be compared to experiences of suffering that make us stronger. The early church would have related this to the persecution they were experiencing.

15:3 clean. This word in Greek is from the same root as that of "prunes" in verse 2. The metaphor is that of being cleansed from sin because of Jesus' death (13:10.)

15:4 produce fruit. Although Paul uses the image of fruit to describe Christian character (Gal. 5:22-23), the fruit here probably relates to 4:35 and 12:24 where a similar agricultural image is used to speak of the many people who would come to Christ. Just as Jesus' fruitfulness was dependent on his doing the Father's will, so the disciple is dependent on holding on to Jesus' teaching.

15:7 ask whatever you want, and it will be done you. Here the promise is in the context of spiritual fruitfulness. See also its counterpart in verse 16.

15:10 If you keep my commands. This is not a reversion to legalism, i.e., "If you do all the right things, I will love you." Rather it's saying that if we expect Christ's (and God's) love, then we need to given Him our obedience. The commands mentioned are probably the two great commandments of loving God with all our heart, soul and mind and loving our neighbor as oneself (Matt. 22:34-40).

15:11 your joy may be complete. God does not call us to obedience to make us miserable, but to give us a joyful, complete life (Neh. 8:10; Rom. 15:13; Gal. 5:22-23).

15:15 friends. The disciples' relationship with Jesus is modeled upon that of Jesus with His Father. In 5:19-20, Jesus said the Father showed Him all that He does. In the same way, Jesus has now revealed to the disciples all that He has learned from the Father.

15:16 whatever you ask the Father in My name, He will give you. This is very similar to what Christ says in Matthew 7:7-8. This is not giving us carte blanche in terms of obtaining material luxury. Rather it is to say that God will provide for all of our needs.

SESSION 2

TELLING OUR STORY

SCRIPTURE: JOHN 4:1-26

In last week's session we saw the importance of staying connected to the vine of Jesus Christ, and considered the role of small groups in helping us to do so. This week we will look at the importance of helping people tell their story. When a person tells their story and feels like they have really been heard, it helps them feel like they are valued and a part of things. In this session we will look at the story of the Samaritan woman at the well in John 4:1-26. We will see how Jesus helped her tell her story and see what we can learn from Him as group leaders.

A small-group leader can bring various areas of expertise to a meeting, including Bible knowledge, good listening skills, and knowledge of group dynamics. But there is one thing that each group participant alone can bring – his or her own personal story. We are enriched by each other's stories, and only when we know the other person's story do we really know them. We do not really know someone simply because we know his or her name. Sharing our stories also helps us to apply Scripture to our life, because then we can see how God has acted in our life in a similar way to how God has acted in the biblical record.

As beneficial as sharing our stories is, it is not always easy. It means becoming a little more vulnerable to each other, and being vulnerable to others can be scary at first. This is easier, however if we do not try to open up to each other all at once, but rather a little at a time. These sessions are designed for members to share a little of their personal lives each time. Through a number of special techniques each member is encouraged to move from low risk less personal sharing to higher risk responses. This helps develop the sense of community and facilitates care giving.

We move from low-risk to higher-risk (and more meaningful) sharing by maintaining six principles in our interaction with each other. These are:

Principle 1: Level the Playing Field: Most of us have had experiences as youth or adults in playing sports. In sports most people do not enjoy playing when they feel the others in the game can play at a much higher level of skill than they can. It's embarrassing when everyone else can knock the ball out of the park and we struggle just to swing the bat without killing ourselves. The same is true in Bible Study experiences. If we are new to the Bible it's not always comfortable for us to be in a group where everyone else seems to know more than we do, and we are afraid of giving a "wrong" answer. What "levels the playing field" in our Serendipity-style groups is that the focus of the core questions is not on academic issues where there are right and wrong answers, and where an in-depth knowledge of the Bible is an advantage; but rather on what the passage means in our own life. How is our own story like the story we are reading in the Bible? In that area we all bring similar expertise.

Principle 2: Share Your Spiritual Story. In sharing about ourselves, we start with sharing about our past, what things were like in our childhood or adolescence. That is easier to do than sharing what we struggle with right now, and it helps us to open up a little more. Before we know it we can easily share with each other about our spiritual journey. It always helps in this process if the one leading is willing to share first, setting an example of openness for the others in the group.

Principle 3: Ask Open-ended Questions. When questions are "yes" or "no" questions, or are questions that can be answered with one short answer, discussion is generally short-circuited. But when questions are asked that encourage people to share in a more open-ended way, then discussion can become spirited, encouraging others to say more. Serendipity material always seeks to use more open-ended questions. An example of a closed question might be, "Did Jesus get in trouble for healing on the Sabbath?" The answer can simply be answered, "Yes." An open-ended question might be, "When did you get in trouble for doing something you thought was right?"

Principle 4: Keep a Three-Part Agenda. Serendipity groups are designed to follow a three-part agenda that provides for increasingly in-depth sharing. Part One is the Icebreaker, where people share less-threatening facts, often about their childhood or adolescence, or their present personal tastes. These always relate to either the subject of the Scriptural text or something that happened to a character in the Scriptural text. Part Two is the Bible Study. In this section we learn the basic facts of the story and compare our own story to the story in the biblical text. The last question or two always requires more vulnerability and has the greatest potential for getting at what the meat of the text is for our own personal life. Part Three is the Caring Time. Here we share our own prayer concerns, and if this is done honestly, it does require a lot of vulnerability. The idea is not to focus on Old Widow Walker in the nursing home, or the starving children in Africa (both legitimate prayer needs in other contexts), but on sharing what our needs are and where we need to grow. These may be harder for us to talk about than the needs of people far away, but we need to share them to grow personally and also to become a caring community with each other. Praying for each other is vital to becoming such a caring community.

Principle 5: Subdivide into Subgroups of 3-6. The larger the group the harder it is to share personal things, especially for the more shy persons in a group. Since we want all to participate, and not just those who naturally like to talk, this subdivision is very important. Also, if you have a group of 10-15 people, it would take quite a long time for everyone to share, and this would make the meetings far too long.

Principle 6: Affirm One Another. People share more easily in an atmosphere they perceive as "safe." It is not a safe environment if you believe people will be critical of you. However, if people in a group affirm what they like about you and what you have to say, for most people, this just opens up the floodgates, and they want to share more and more. Such affirmation should always be sincere, and well thought-out, and it is best modeled by the one who is the leader. Most Serendipity groups build in times where such affirmation is encouraged, but it can be done at any point in a meeting when you as leader want to encourage something that has happened or something that has been said.

Utilizing these principles in a group will help that group move much more easily in the direction of caring self-disclosure.

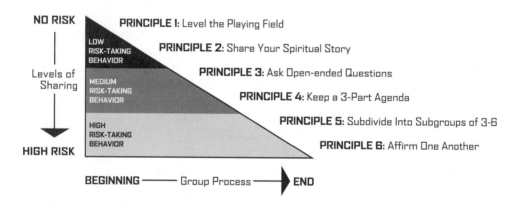

ICEBREAKER

Connect with your Group | **15 Min.**

***LEADER

In order to give each person being trained as a leader experience in leading, assign a different member of the group each week to lead this Icebreaker. In leading the Icebreaker it is important to go around in the circle and have each person share in turn. To do this section, subdivide your group into groups of three to six persons. To help your group members get acquainted, have each person introduce him or herself and then take turns answering all three of the Icebreaker questions. Be sure that everyone gets a chance to participate.

We all like to belong, but most of us have known some times when it felt like we did not. Often those times occur when we are teens. Sometimes we were excluded. Sometimes we did the excluding. What about you? By answering the following questions, share your own experience with being the one on the inside or being the one on the outside looking in.

1. What was the favorite hangout of you and your friends when you were a teenager? What did you like to do there?

2. Who was the least likely to exclude you when you were a teen?
   • other races
   • "Goths"

- rednecks
- the rich kids
- the popular crowd
- non-Christians
- the druggies
- Christians
- the jocks
- other _____.

3. As a teen, what person was most likely to accept you when nobody else would?

 BIBLE STUDY   *Read Scripture and Discuss* | **30 Min.**

In every society there are those who nobody takes time to listen to. In the Israel of Jesus' day, men didn't listen to women, and Israelites didn't listen to Samaritans. That is why it is especially significant that in the following passage Jesus listens to the story of a Samaritan woman. In listening to her he showed her that he cared about her as a person. Even when he knew the darkest aspects of her story, he didn't judge her. Rather he accepted her. That is what we aspire to in small group life. Not everyone has a "dark past" like this woman, but most of us do have aspects of ourselves which make us wonder if others would accept us if they knew all about us. When people do know about us and accept us anyway, it is incredibly freeing. As you read this passage, consider what a difference being heard made in this woman's life.

Narrator: [1] When Jesus knew that the Pharisees heard He was making and baptizing more disciples than John [2] (though Jesus Himself was not baptizing, but His disciples were), [3] He left Judea and went again to Galilee. [4] He had to travel through Samaria, [5] so He came to a town of Samaria called Sychar near the property that Jacob had given his son Joseph. [6] Jacob's well was there, and Jesus, worn out from His journey, sat down at the well. It was about six in the evening. [7] A woman of Samaria came to draw water.

Jesus: "Give Me a drink," Jesus said to her,

Narrator: [8] for His disciples had gone into town to buy food.

Woman: [9] "How is it that You, a Jew, ask for a drink from me, a Samaritan woman?"

she asked.

Narrator: For Jews do not associate with Samaritans.

Jesus: [10] Jesus answered, "If you knew the gift of God, and who is saying to you, 'Give Me a drink,' you would ask Him, and He would give you living water."

Woman: [11] "Sir," said the woman, "You don't even have a bucket, and the well is deep. So where do you get this 'living water'? [12] You aren't greater than our father Jacob, are you? He gave us the well and drank from it himself, as did his sons and livestock."

Jesus: [13] Jesus said, "Everyone who drinks from this water will get thirsty again. [14] But whoever drinks from the water that I will give him will never get thirsty again—ever! In fact, the water I will give him will become a well of water springing up within him for eternal life."

Woman: [15] "Sir," the woman said to Him, "give me this water so I won't get thirsty and come here to draw water."

Jesus: [16] "Go call your husband," He told her, "and come back here."

Woman: [17] "I don't have a husband," she answered.

Jesus: "You have correctly said, 'I don't have a husband,' " Jesus said. [18] "For you've had five husbands, and the man you now have is not your husband. What you have said is true."

Woman: [19] "Sir," the woman replied, "I see that You are a prophet. [20] Our fathers worshiped on this mountain, yet you Jews say that the place to worship is in Jerusalem."

Jesus: [21] Jesus told her, "Believe Me, woman, an hour is coming when you will worship the Father neither on this mountain nor in Jerusalem. [22] You Samaritans worship what you do not know. We worship what we do know, because salvation is from the Jews. [23] But an hour is coming, and is now here, when the true worshipers will worship the Father in spirit and truth. Yes, the Father wants such people to worship Him. [24] God is Spirit, and those who worship Him must worship in spirit and truth."

Woman: [25] The woman said to Him, "I know that Messiah is coming" (who is called

Christ). "When He comes, He will explain everything to us."

Jesus: ²⁶ "I am He," Jesus told her, "the One speaking to you."

John 4:1-26

 # QUESTIONS FOR INTERACTION

***LEADER

Divide the group into subgroups of three to six persons each, and assign someone to lead each subgroup. It is best to assign people who did not have the chance to lead last week.

Refer to the Summary and Study Notes at the end of this section as needed. If 30 minutes is not enough time to answer all of the questions in this section, conclude the Bible Study by answering questions 6 and 7.

1. When was the last time that you struck up a conversation with a stranger in a manner similar to what Jesus does here? Is it easy or difficult for you to talk to strangers in such a situation? What "serendipity" (the property of making joyous, providential discoveries unexpectedly) have you experienced in such a conversation?

2. Why is the woman surprised by the fact that Jesus asks her for a drink of water? Do you think he has any other motivation for asking for this, other than his thirst?

3. What does Jesus mean by "living water"? How does the woman misunderstand what he was trying to say with this phrase?

4. Why does Jesus bring up this touchy issue of the woman's husband? How does she respond to his knowledge of her marital history?

5. What would you say is the most important thing that Jesus says about proper worship? How satisfied do you think this woman would have been with how he dealt with this controversial issue of worship locale?

6. Jesus helped this woman talk about a dark part of her life, her marital history. Which of the following most helps you to talk about difficult episodes in your own life story?
   · When others in the group are similarly vulnerable.
   · When people are accepting like Jesus was.
   · Knowing God has forgiven all of my mistakes.
   · When people respect confidentiality.
   · Laughing together makes it easier to share such serious stuff.
   · I have difficulty ever sharing such things.
   · other _____.

7. With whom is it more easy for you to open up and share – complete strangers, as in this encounter at the well, or people whom you see a lot? What makes each easier or more difficult?

 GOING DEEPER: *If your group has time and/or wants a challenge, go on to this question.*

8. In what way does asking someone to help us, as Jesus did when he asked for the water, open up a relationship?

9. What do you learn from this story about breaking down barriers between people who are from cultural groups that are hostile to each other?

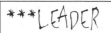 **CARING TIME** Apply the Lesson & Pray for One another   **15 Min.**

1. Who do you know who are the rejected Samaritan women (and men) of your church? Include a prayer for them.

2. Pray that God will help your group toward greater openness with each other.

3. What "cup of water" (a word of encouragement or a little act to refresh you on your journey) can this group give to you right now?

NEXT WEEK

Today we considered how to help someone tell their story, by focusing on the biblical story of Jesus and the Samaritan woman. Next week we will learn to appreciate the importance of affirmation in group work by looking at the way Paul affirmed his readers. Make sure that you read the small Introduction section at the beginning of Session Two prior to the session.

NOTES ON JOHN 4:1-26

Summary: It is clear that Jesus widened the circle of who could be included in the family of faith. The traditional religious leaders of the days, the scribes, Pharisees and Sadducees, wanted to exclude Gentiles, Samaritans, the blind and disabled, and even women. All of these were seen as a little less worthy of God than they were. But Jesus consistently loved and taught the ones these religious leaders wouldn't even talk to. In this story He talks to a Samaritan woman, who would have been in the eyes of most Jewish men the lowest of the low. Not only does He talk to her, but even though He knows of her dark past, He does not condemn her. He is just as open to her and her questions as He is to his Jewish male disciples.

4:1-3 The Pharisees had already investigated John (1:24-27), and the other Gospels make clear their opposition to him because of his challenge to their position (Matt. 3:7-10; Mark 11:27-33). Jesus' popularity undoubtedly fueled their suspicions as well.

4:4 Samaria. This was a territory sandwiched between the provinces of Judea and Galilee. When the northern kingdom of Israel was conquered in 722 B.C. by the Assyrians, many of its people were deported, and exiles from other areas of the vast Assyrian Empire were brought in (2 Kings 17:22-41). Many of these people intermarried with the remaining Israelites and adopted some of the Jewish religious practices. In Jesus' day strict Jews would avoid Samaria as an unclean area, and the term "Samaritan" was used as an insult (8:48).

4:5 near the property that Jacob had given. Genesis 48:22 tells of Jacob giving some land to Joseph.

4:6 six in the evening. Literally, this is "the sixth hour." Since the day began at sunrise, most translators equate this with about noon.

4:7 came to draw water. Noontime, the heat of the day, was not the normal time women would perform this chore. Six in the evening, the way the Holman Christian Standard Bible translates verse 6, would be more normal, which may be why it was translated that way. However, since we later learn that this woman had been married many times, she may have been subject to much gossip, which would be a reason she might have come at noon, to avoid other women. "Will you give me a drink?" Asking someone for something makes you dependent on them, which is part of the reason why a Jewish man would not normally make such a request of a Samaritan woman. By making himself vulnerable in this way, however, Jesus lets her know that she is needed, and this encourages relationship.

4:9 Jews do not associate with Samaritans. Since some strands of Judaism regarded Samaritans as unclean from birth, Jesus' request shocks the woman. Rabbi Eliezer ben Hyrcanus, a second century rabbi said, "He that eats the bread of the Samaritans is like to one that eats the flesh of swine."

4:10 living water. This was a common phrase meaning water that flowed from a river or spring. Water like this had better quality that the standing water of a well or pond. Jesus, however, means much more than this. He is referring to a refreshment of the soul that brings spiritual life in the same way that water brings physical life.

4:11-12 The woman takes Jesus words about living water as an insult to the quality of water in the well. She essentially says, "Since this water was good enough for Jacob, who are you that you think it's not good enough for you?"

4:14 a well of water springing up. This is the same word translated as "well" in verse 6. By this play on words the author presents us with a picture of two fountains or wells. Jesus' "well" forever quenches spiritual thirst.

4:17-18 While clearly revealing his knowledge of her situation, Jesus commends her truthfulness. Women in this time could be divorced for trivial reasons, but had no right of divorce themselves. It is also possible that she had simply been abandoned by one or more of her husbands and was simply a mistress to the man she was with now – she was considered immoral. Still, Jesus does not reject or condemn her. This encourages her to learn more about Him.

4:19 prophet. Jesus' knowledge of her led her to see Him as a prophet who must be taken seriously. The Samaritans did not acknowledge the Jewish prophets and writings, but held only to the five books of Moses.

4:23 an hour is coming, and is now here. This captures the tension of this Gospel's announcement about the kingdom of God. It is both present and future. true worshipers. The barrier between Jewish and Samaritan religion is dismissed. Their concern about location indicates that both have missed the point.

4:24 God is Spirit. As Spirit, God cannot be limited to living in a house, like the temple, or a shrine, of which there were a variety in Samaria. Since God is beyond one limited location, the location where one worships shouldn't matter either.

SESSION 3

AFFIRMING ONE ANOTHER

SCRIPTURE: PHILIPPIANS 1:3-11

Last week we considered how to help someone tell their story, by focusing on the biblical story of Jesus and the Samaritan woman. This week we will learn to appreciate the importance of affirmation in group work by looking at the way Paul affirmed his readers. In almost every letter he wrote he included something he could praise God about in what that church was doing. What he wrote in Philippians 1:3–11 is a prime example.

Make sure that each participant reads and studies this section prior to this session.

Whether it be in our profession or in the way we live our life, most of us are much more conscious of what we are doing wrong than we are of what we are doing right. Our mistakes loom large in our memory and they seek to bring us down to discouragement and despair. That is why it is so important to have a supportive community around us to remind us of what is good about us and what we have done right. Such affirmations rejuvenate us and help us to believe in ourselves so that we try even harder in the future.

As small-group leaders it is essential that we help our group be an affirming group. Some of this is done through the material we use, and that is why Serendipity makes conscious efforts to build in affirmation opportunities into our small-group material. However, it is also important that the group leader be conscious of the need for affirmation and that he or she model such affirmation. Modeling affirmation takes it from the theoretical (which is nice, but which can be ignored) to the practical and real. In modeling such affirmation, here are some points we need to keep in mind:

- **Affirmation should be sincere**. Everyone has something about them that is real that can be affirmed. We do not have to make things up or say things that we know are not true. False affirmation is worse than no affirmation because it says to the person, "It is so difficult finding something good about you that I have to make something up!"

- **Affirmation should not be manipulative**. We affirm people because it helps them feel good about themselves, and because it encourages the positive behaviors which we affirm. But we should not use affirmation to manipulate people, or to use them for our own purposes. That is the difference between true affirmation and flattery.

- **Affirmation does not mean back-handed compliments**. It is not affirming to say, "Well, it's good to see that you are not as boring as you were when you taught that class last summer!" A good test of an affirmation is, "How would I feel if someone told me this?"

- **Affirmation should be done regularly**. We do not affirm someone once and then think we are done with that for the rest of the relationship. Affirmation is like food and drink to us. No matter how good it is, one meal will not last a lifetime. Leaders should seek regular opportunities to affirm group members and to encourage them to affirm each other.

- **Affirmation should be done to God's glory**. When we affirm each other, we also thank God for what God has done in that other person. We do not affirm someone as part of idolizing them or lifting them in importance over others. Rather we are affirming that God is doing something important and beautiful through them.

If our groups affirm each other in the ways outlined above, group members will feel good about who they are, and they will look forward to what the group does together. This will give your group a vitality and spirit that will make it powerful!

ICEBREAKER   *Connect with your Group* | **15 Min.**

***LEADER**

Remember to assign a different member of the group each week to lead this Icebreaker. In leading the Icebreaker it is important to go around in the circle and have each person share in turn. To do this section, subdivide your group into groups of three to six persons. To help your group members get acquainted, have each person take turns answering all three of the Icebreaker questions.

Sometimes we talk as if emphasizing the positive with people and avoiding negativism is some kind of modern psychological ploy. However, Paul used such a positive approach with the churches he founded nearly two millennia ago. He always remembered to thank them for what they were doing for the Lord. Still, some of us have not learned the wisdom of this approach. We ignore what people do right and jump on their case for what they do wrong. What about you? How do you do with sharing a positive word of thanks with the people around you? Share something of your approach to thanking people by answering the following questions.

1. If you could pick just one person from your childhood to thank God for, other than persons in your immediate family, who would it be? What would you especially thank God for in this person?

2. How good are you generally at saying "thanks" to those who have done special things for you?
   - I don't know — I've never done it before.
   - I generally have to be reminded.
   - I thank people for the big stuff.
   - I always remember to thank people.
   - I even thank people for thanking me — and thank you for this question.

3. What have people done for you in this past week that you thank God for?

BIBLE STUDY *Read Scripture and Discuss* | **30 Min.**

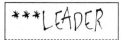

Select a person from your group to read the following passage from Philippians 1:3-11

Paul was a prolific letter writer, and his letters almost always started out the same way — he thanked God for the people to whom he was writing. His letter to the Philippians is perhaps the best example of this because this church held such a special place in his heart. Looking at what he wrote reminds us of how important it is to affirm the people we care about and the relationship we have with them.

³ I give thanks to my God for every remembrance of you, ⁴ always praying with joy for all of you in my every prayer, ⁵ because of your partnership in the gospel from the first day until now. ⁶ I am sure of this, that He who started a good work in you will carry it on to completion until the day of Christ Jesus. ⁷ It is right for me to think this way about all of you, because I have you in my heart, and you are all partners with me in grace, both in my imprisonment and in the defense and establishment of the gospel. ⁸ For God is my witness, how I deeply miss all of you with the affection of Christ Jesus. ⁹ And I pray this: that your love will keep on growing in knowledge and every kind of discernment, ¹⁰ so that you can determine what really matters and can be pure and blameless in the day of Christ, ¹¹ filled with the fruit of righteousness that Îcomes° through Jesus Christ, to the glory and praise of God.

Philippians 1:3-11

QUESTIONS FOR INTERACTION

***LEADER

Divide the group into subgroups of three to six persons each, and assign someone to lead each subgroup.

Refer to the Summary and Study Notes at the end of this section as needed. If 30 minutes is not enough time to answer all of the questions in this section, conclude the Bible Study by answering questions 6 and 7.

1. Who in your life do you miss with the same intensity that Paul speaks of missing the Christians of Philippi?

2. Why do you think Paul is so confident that God will carry on to completion the work he started through the Philippians? Is this a statement of confidence in God, a statement of confidence in the Philippians or both?

3. In what ways were the Philippians in "partnership" with Paul in the work he was doing (see Notes on verses 5 and 7)?

4. How does one become "pure and blameless" according to verses 9-11 (see Notes)?

5. Of the things for which Paul prays for the Philippians, which do you most feel the need for?
   • a greater ability to love (v.9)
   • a greater ability to discern "what really matters" (vv. 9-10)
   • to be "pure and blameless" (v.10) – guilt really gets to me!
   • to live a more fruitful life (v.11)

6. What work has God started in you that you really want to make sure is carried on to completion?

7. Who more than anyone else has "partnered" with you in your spiritual development? How has this person helped you grow?

GOING DEEPER: *If your group has time and/or wants a challenge, go on to these questions.*

8. Some people avoid thanking others or saying positive things about them out of fear the person will "get a big head" or "rest on their laurels". How would you respond to that perspective, especially in light of what Paul does here?

9. What is the relative importance of thanking God for what He has done through people, and thanking the people themselves?

CARING TIME *Apply the Lesson & Pray for One another* **15 Min.**

***LEADER

Remember, this very important time is for developing and expressing your concern for each other as group members by praying for one another. Bring the group members back together and begin the Caring Time by sharing responses to all three questions. In this session, ask for two volunteers to pray for the concerns mentioned by group members.

1. Take time to pray for the completion of the work you mentioned in question 6. How can this group be supportive of you in this venture?

2. What do you thank God for in the other persons in this group? Focus on one group member at a time and have the others share what they are thankful for about that person. After everyone has had a chance to share about each person, go on to the next.

3. What is happening in the group as a whole that you would like to thank God for?

NEXT WEEK

Today we looked at the importance Paul placed on affirming people, and we took some time to affirm one another. This process of affirmation should not stop with this lesson, but should be integrated into each session as people experience things they are thankful for. Next week we will consider what it means that God has given us spiritual gifts, and we will see what importance they have to small group leadership. We will do this by looking at 1 Corinthians 12: 7-31. As always, make sure that you read the small Introduction section at the beginning of next week's session prior to the session.

Summary: In a typical Greek letter, following the salutation, a prayer was offered on behalf of the recipients. Paul follows the custom here, as he does in most of his letters. Specifically, he thanks God for the long partnership he has had with the Philippians. He expresses his gratitude (vv. 3-6) and his affection for them (vv.7-8). Then he describes his prayer for them.

1:3 for every remembrance of you. This is a difficult phrase to translate from the Greek. What it seems to mean is that Paul gave thanks for them regularly.

1:4 my every prayer. This is not the usual Greek word for prayer. (That word is found in verse 9.) This is a word that carries the idea of "need" or "lack," and so came to mean intercessory prayer. Paul is not just praying in general for the Philippians. He is praying that God will meet specific needs that he knows they have. **with joy**. "Joy" is a theme that pervades Philippians. This is the first of some 14 times that Paul will use the word in this epistle. He mentions "joy" more often in this short epistle than in any of his other letters. It is interesting that his first reference to joy is in connection with prayer.

1:5 because of your partnership. Paul is grateful to God for the Philippians, because they have always stood by him in the work of the gospel. The Greek word rendered here as "partnership" is the familiar word koinonia, translated elsewhere as "fellowship." It means, literally, "having something in common." It is a favorite word of Paul's. Of the 19 times it appears in the New Testament, he uses it 13 times. **in the gospel**. The Philippians were partners with Paul in spreading the gospel. Specifically, they supported him financially in his ministry (2:25;

4:10-20). In addition, they worked with him to spread the gospel (4:3); they prayed for him (1:19); and they contributed generously to the fund he raised in aid of the needy Christians in Jerusalem (2 Cor. 8:1-5). The word "gospel" is another favorite of Paul's. He uses it 60 of the 76 times it appears in the New Testament. The "gospel" is the good news about what God has done in Christ Jesus to save men and women.

1:6 I am sure of this. Confidence is another of the underlying themes of Philippians. Paul makes it very clear what lies at the root of this confidence. It is not human accomplishment or ritual of any sort (3:3-4). This is confidence that springs out of faith in who God is and what He is doing. **the day of Christ Jesus**. This is the moment when Christ will return in glory and triumph to establish His kingdom on earth.

1:7 because I have you in my heart. The phrase could equally well be translated, as in the NEB, "because you hold me in such affection." In this case, the way Paul feels about the Philippians is based on their affection for him. Perhaps the phrase is intended to be ambiguous and to be read both ways, since there was a mutuality of affection between Paul and the Philippians. **partners with me in grace**. They are partners with Paul both in the receiving of

God's grace and in the dispensing of it. **In the defense and the establishment of the gospel**. These are legal terms. The reference is to Paul's defense before the Roman court, in which he hopes to be able not only to vindicate himself and the gospel from false charges, but to proclaim the gospel in life-changing power to those in the courtroom. (See Acts 26 for an example of how Paul did this when he stood in court before Agrippa and Festus.)

1:8 God is my witness. In moments of deep feeling, Paul would sometimes invoke God to bear witness to the authenticity of these feelings (see also Rom. 1:9; 2 Cor. 11:11, 31; 1 Thess. 2:5). **I deeply miss**. Yet another word characteristic of Paul. He uses it seven of the nine times it is found in the New Testament. This is a strong word and expresses the depth of Paul's feelings for them, his desire to be with them, and wish to minister to them.

1:9 And I pray this. Paul's love for the Philippians leads him to prayer on their behalf. What he prays is that they will overflow with love. He prays that this love will increase (i.e., that it will go on developing) and that it will be regulated by knowledge and discernment.

1:10 so that you can determine what really matters. The Philippians are confronted with competing ideologies as to what is true and how to live. They need "knowledge" and "insight" in order to choose and follow that which is of God and so results in "purity" and blamelessness." The word translated "determine" is used to describe the process of testing coins so as to distinguish between those that are real and those that are counterfeit. **pure and blameless**. No one is pure and blameless on their own merit, except Jesus Christ alone. However, when we have faith in Jesus Christ, that faith is counted as righteousness or moral purity (see Rom. 4.) Here this truth is expressed in verse 11, where we are told that this "fruit of righteousness comes through Jesus Christ."

SESSION 4

FINDING OUR GIFTEDNESS

SCRIPTURE: 1 CORINTHIANS 12:7-31

Last week we looked at the importance Paul placed on affirming people, and we took some time to affirm one another. We should continue to seek opportunities to affirm each other in this session and in sessions to come. This week, as we look at 1 Corinthians 12:7-31, we will consider what it means that God has given us spiritual gifts, and we will see what importance they have to small group leadership. Affirming such gifts is a vital task of a small-group leader.

Part of the role of a small-group leader is to assess the gifts of group members, both for helping lead the present group and also to develop group leadership for future groups. As your group matures through the Growth and Develop Stages, the present leadership team should identify apprentice leaders and facilitators. This is done best in a small group setting. Look for an engineer type as the group administrator, the party animal as the hospitality person or party leader, a person that loves inter-action and knowledge as the facilitator and a caring person to handle group shep-herding. Here are some instructions on what each needs to do:

Coordinator/ Group Administrator: Is responsible to the church leadership team for:
1. Building a leadership team.
2. Ensuring the coordination of the group.
3. Meeting with the leadership team once a month for encouragement and planning.
4. Casting a vision for multiplication and beginning the process of multiplication.

Facilitator: Is responsible to the coordinator for:
1. Guiding the group in life-changing Bible study.
2. Developing a facilitating team for subgrouping into groups of three to six.
3. Keeping the group on agenda, but being sensitive when someone needs to share.
4. Subdividing the group for Bible study and caring time and emphasizing the "empty chair."

Care Leader: Is responsible to the coordinator for:
1. Contacting group members to encourage attendance and personal growth.
2. Keeping the group informed of prayer needs.
3. Coordinating caring for the special needs of the group.

Child Care Coordinator
1. Be responsible for having someone to care for younger children.
2. Plan any special activities or training for children.
3. Select any material necessary for working with children.

Party Leader: Is responsible to the coordinator for:
1. Planning, coordinating and promoting monthly group parties.
2. Keeping the members involved in the party activities.

Host/Hostess: Is responsible to the coordinator for:
1. Providing a clean home with enough space to subdivide into groups of three to six.
2. Coordinating refreshments.
3. Welcoming guests and having name tags at each meeting.
4. Making sure everything is conducive for sharing (no TV, comfortable temperature, arrangements for children).

After you have selected these leaders, you must seek to train and mentor them as they grow in confidence. Here is an outline of this process:
   a. Identify apprentice leaders and facilitators
   b. Provide on-the-job training
   c. Give them the opportunity to lead your group
   d. Introduce the new team to your church or your small-group leadership team
   e. Launch the new group

| **ICEBREAKER** | Connect with your Group | **15 Min.** |

***LEADER

Remember to assign a different member of the group each week to lead this Icebreaker. In leading the Icebreaker it is important to go around in the circle and have each person share in turn.

To help your group members get acquainted, have each person take turns answering all three of the Icebreaker questions.

Sometimes we refer to certain people as "talented people." But as we will see this week in our Scriptural reading, all of us have been given talents. Sometimes they are talents that the rest of the world does not pay attention to, but all of us have been given talents. The question is what we do with our talents. Do we ignore them, put them down, use them to go on an ego trip, or use them for God? How do you relate to your own talents? Share something of your own style through the following questions.

1. In which of the following areas would you have considered yourself gifted when you were in school?
   • math
   • reading & writing
   • sports

- science
- shop
- music
- drama
- making friends
- shopping
- brown-nosing the teachers
- skipping school
- babysitting
- other _____.

2. Finish this sentence: "When I was a teenager the person who most encouraged me to develop my talents was…"

3. When you are good at something are you most likely to…
- let people know it.
- drive myself to be even better.
- take personal pride in my accomplishments.
- dismiss my talent as unimportant.
- envy those with talents in other areas.
- put down those who don't do it as well.
- other _____.

 BIBLE STUDY   *Read Scripture and Discuss* | **30 Min.**

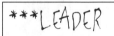 ***LEADER

Select a person from your group to read the following passages from 1 Corinthians 12: 7-31.

It seems that every society values certain gifts or talents over others. In our society the most valued talents are the ability to sing and dance, act or play sports. In ancient Corinth they became fascinated with the gift some people had to speak in strange, heavenly languages. In their minds this was the pinnacle of gifts and there could be nothing greater. But Paul set them straight by outlining a variety of gifts, all of which are needed in different ways. Then he went on in 1 Corinthians 13 to say that the greatest gift of all was not tongues, but love. Here in chapter 12 he contents himself to point out that all gifts are needed and they all work together like the different members of a body. As you read this passage, think of how your own gifts fit in with the rest of the body.

[7] A manifestation of the Spirit is given to each person to produce what is beneficial:
[8] to one is given a message of wisdom through the Spirit,
  to another, a message of knowledge by the same Spirit,

⁹ to another, faith by the same Spirit,
  to another, gifts of healing by the one Spirit,
¹⁰ to another, the performing of miracles,
  to another, prophecy,
  to another, distinguishing between spirits,
  to another, different kinds of languages,
  to another, interpretation of languages.
¹¹ But one and the same Spirit is active in all these, distributing to each one as He wills.
¹² For as the body is one and has many parts, and all the parts of that body, though many, are one body—so also is Christ. ¹³ For we were all baptized by one Spirit into one body—whether Jews or Greeks, whether slaves or free—and we were all made to drink of one Spirit. ¹⁴ So the body is not one part but many. ¹⁵ If the foot should say, "Because I'm not a hand, I don't belong to the body," in spite of this it still belongs to the body. ¹⁶ And if the ear should say, "Because I'm not an eye, I don't belong to the body," in spite of this it still belongs to the body. ¹⁷ If the whole body were an eye, where would the hearing be? If the whole were an ear, where would be the sense of smell? ¹⁸ But now God has placed the parts, each one of them, in the body just as He wanted. ¹⁹ And if they were all the same part, where would the body be? ²⁰ Now there are many parts, yet one body.

²¹ So the eye cannot say to the hand, "I don't need you!" nor again the head to the feet, "I don't need you!" ²² On the contrary, all the more, those parts of the body that seem to be weaker are necessary. ²³ And those parts of the body that we think to be less honorable, we clothe these with greater honor, and our unpresentable parts have a better presentation. ²⁴ But our presentable parts have no need Îof clothingˆ. Instead, God has put the body together, giving greater honor to the less honorable, ²⁵ so that there would be no division in the body, but that the members would have the same concern for each other. ²⁶ So if one member suffers, all the members suffer with it; if one member is honored, all the members rejoice with it.

²⁷ Now you are the body of Christ, and individual members of it. ²⁸ And God has placed these in the church:
  first apostles, second prophets, third teachers, next, miracles,
  then gifts of healing, helping, managing, various kinds of languages.
²⁹ Are all apostles? Are all prophets?
  Are all teachers? Do all do miracles?
³⁰ Do all have gifts of healing? Do all speak in languages? Do all interpret?
³¹ But desire the greater gifts. And I will show you an even better way.

1 Corinthians 12:7-31

QUESTIONS FOR INTERACTION

***LEADER

Divide the group into subgroups of three to six persons each, and assign someone to lead each subgroup.

Refer to the Summary and Study Notes at the end of this section as needed. If 30 minutes is not enough time to answer all of the questions in this section, conclude the Bible Study by answering questions 7 and 8.

1. If you were a part of the body, which part would you be?
   - an ear – because I am a good listener.
   - an eye – because I am very observant of what is happening around me.
   - a foot – because I am always going somewhere
   - a hand – because I love to mold things and to create
   - a mouth – because I enjoy talking.
   - a pair of shoulders – because I often shoulder the load wherever I am
   - a head – because I enjoy mental challenges
   - a heart – because I am all feelings.

2. According to this passage, who is in charge of distributing various gifts to people? Why are people given these gifts?

3. In what way is the church like a body? What does this body-image say about the unity of the church?

4. What do verses 14-20 say about envying the gifts of others?

5. After reading verses 21-26, what would you say would be the problem with trying to be a "Lone Ranger"-style Christian?

6. What are the implications of verse 26 for small groups like this one and the ones you will be leading? What needs to happen in order for us to do the best possible job of suffering and rejoicing with each other?

7. When have you felt like you really weren't part of a church fellowship because you were different than the other "body parts"? What happened that made you feel you were different? What could have been done to better draw you in?

8. What gift do you believe the Spirit has given you to "produce what is beneficial" for Christ and His church? How well do you think you are utilizing that gift right now?

GOING DEEPER: *If your group has time and/or wants a challenge, go on to this question.*

9. What gifts do you believe the church is neglecting right now? How can we better utilize people who have these gifts?

10. Are all the gifts that a person might have listed in this chapter (vv. 7-10, 28-30)? Support your answer (for other lists of gifts, see Rom. 12:6-8; Eph. 4:11-16).

CARING TIME *Apply the Lesson & Pray for One another* | **15 Min.**

***LEADER

Once again, use this time to develop and express your concern for each other as group members by praying for one another. Bring the group back together and begin the Caring Time by sharing responses to all three questions. In this session, encourage group members to pray at will before you close. First have group members answer the following questions.

1. How have you seen other group members manifesting the gift they have through the Spirit during the course of these sessions together? Share on this at will. Take note of these gifts and take time to thank God for them.

2. What can this group rejoice with you about this week?

3. In what way are you suffering? How can this group share with you in this suffering through prayer this week?

NEXT WEEK

Today we looked at what it means to receive spiritual gifts, and we considered the specific gifts we have all been given. We noted how a small group can utilize gifts and also affirm the oneness of the body of Christ by sharing in our joys and sorrows. Next week we will look at a somewhat different aspect of group life — what it means to admonish one another. Can we do this without crossing over into self-righteousness or judgmentalism? We will face this challenging issue by looking at an encounter between Apollos and the husband-wife team of Priscilla and Aquila. As always, make sure that you read the small Introduction section at the beginning of next week's session prior to the session.

Summary: The world has always been full of people who have felt left out and unappreciated. In this passage from 1 Corinthians, Paul makes it clear that such should not happen in the church. The Holy Spirit has given everyone a gift that can be used for the common benefit, and thus we all need each other. We are to work together like the various parts of the human body work together in order to live and grow. No part of the body can function alone. No part of the body is unneeded. This message was important in a church which thought that only speaking in heavenly languages was a valued gift.

12:7 to each person. Every Christian has a spiritual gift. **to produce what is beneficial**. The purpose of these gifts is not private advantage, but community growth. The NIV translates this "for the common good."

12:8–10 Paul illustrates the variety of gifts. By chapter 14 it will have become clear that he stresses this point because the Corinthians had become preoccupied, to their detriment, with a single gift—tongues or languages.

12:8 through the Spirit. Paul again emphasizes the supernatural origins of these gifts. **wisdom / knowledge**. It is not clear how (or if) these gifts differ. Perhaps a message of wisdom focused on practical, ethical instruction, while a message of knowledge involved exposition of biblical truth. In either case, the emphasis is on the actual discourse given for the benefit of the assembled Christians.

12:9 faith. To trust in God's power to do seemingly impossible things. Saving faith, which all Christians share, is not in view here. **healing**. Special ability to effect miraculous cures. Paul apparently had this gift (Acts 14:8–10).

12:10 performing of miracles. Probably the gift of exorcism and similar types of confrontation with evil supernatural powers. **prophecy**. Inspired utterances given in ordinary (not ecstatic) speech, distinguished from teaching and wisdom by its unpremeditated nature. **distinguishing between spirits**. Just because a person claimed to be inspired by the Holy Spirit did not make it true. Those who possessed this gift of discernment were able to identify the source of an utterance—whether it came from the Holy Spirit or another spirit. **different kinds of languages**. Ecstatic speech, unintelligible except by those with the gift of interpretation of these languages. **interpretation of languages**. This gift allowed a person to understand and explain to others what was being said by someone else in a divine language.

12:11 Paul underscores his main point: the gifts are given by the Spirit's choice and for His purposes. Hence, they are not a sign of spiritual attainment.

12:12 is one and has many parts. This is Paul's central point in verses 12–30: "diversity within unity." **so also is Christ**. The church is the body of Christ (v. 27), and so indeed Christ can be understood to be made up of many parts. Yet He is also the Lord (v. 3), and thus head over that church.

12:13 Here Paul points to the unity side of the body of Christ. Unity exists because all were baptized into one Spirit, and all drink from one Spirit. His concern is not with how people become believers, but with how believers become one body. The way believers are immersed in the Spirit is like baptism. **baptized by one Spirit**. Paul's concern here is not with the means by which believers are baptized, but with the common reality in which all believers exist; i.e., the Holy Spirit. **made to drink of one Spirit**. Paul continues speaking metaphorically, with the idea of water still dominant. Being incorporated into one body is not only like baptism, it is also like "drinking the same Spirit."

12:14 Now Paul points to the diversity side of the body of Christ (which is his major concern): the one body has many different parts to it.

12:17 If all Christians had the same gift, the body would be impoverished.

12:21 Each part of the body needs the other parts. No one gift (tongues) can stand alone. Wholeness in the body requires that all the parts function together.

12:22 weaker. An organ's size or physical strength is not necessarily an indication of its importance. Human achievement in comparison to animals has been due in part to the fact that humans have an opposable thumb. Internal organs that are delicate are essential to life.

12:26 In fact, the whole person suffers when one sprains an ankle. It is not just the ankle that suffers.

12:27 Paul sums up the meaning of his metaphor. **the body of Christ**. By this phrase, Paul conveys the idea not that Christ consists of this body, but that Christ rules over this body, and that this body belongs to him.

12:28 Paul offers a second list of the types of gifts given by the Holy Spirit (see the parallel list in Eph. 4:11)—mixing together ministries (apostles) with spiritual gifts (the gift of healing). **apostles**. These individuals were responsible for founding new churches. They were pioneer church planters. **prophets**. Those who were inspired to speak God's word to the church, in plain (not ecstatic) language. **teachers**. Those gifted to instruct others in the meaning of the Christian faith and its implications for one's life. **then**. Having first focused on those gifts whereby the church is established and nurtured, Paul then shifts to other gifts. **helping**. The gift of support; those whose function it was to aid the needy (the poor, the widow, the orphan). **managing**. The gift of direction (literally, the process of steering a ship through the rocks and safely to shore); those whose function it was to guide church affairs.

12:29–30 While Paul does not rule out the possibility that a particular individual might possess more than one gift, he is quite clear that no one has all the gifts. The implied answer to each question is "No."

12:31 the greater gifts. These are the gifts which edify the church most. Paul establishes the context within which all gifts should function: love, which is the more excellent way.

SESSION 5

GIVING MUTUAL ADMONITION

SCRIPTURE: ACTS 18:18-28

Last week we looked at what it means to receive spiritual gifts, we considered the specific gifts we have all been given, and we noted how a small group can affirm and utilize these gifts. This week we will look at a somewhat different aspect of group life — what it means to admonish one another. Can we do this without crossing over into self-righteousness or judgmentalism? People will share in a small-group setting only if they feel they can do so without being judged, and that is why in these groups we do not give unsolicited advice. And yet there are times we may feel the need to encourage someone to re-think their position on some issue. We will consider this challenging issue by looking at an encounter between Apollos and the husband-wife team of Priscilla and Aquila.

Christians who want to follow the dictates of Scripture sometimes face a dilemma when it comes to talking to other Christians about their beliefs or behavior. On the one hand Jesus taught that we should not seek to take the "speck" out of the eye of our brother or sister when we have a "log" in our own eye (see Matt. 7:1-5.) On the other hand, we are told to "admonish" one another (Col. 3:16; Titus 3:10-11), and we have the example of this week's Scripture where Priscilla and Aquila correct Apollos on a matter of doctrine. What are we to do? One of the problems we face is that we often can see another person's "mistakes" more clearly than our own. This can lead to a person spending all their energy on "fixing" everyone else instead of correcting his or her own behavior. In Serendipity groups we encourage a covenant that prohibits giving unsolicited advice. This does not mean that we feel there is never a need for Christians to challenge each other's ideas or behavior. However, in the context of building a small group community, several points are important:

- **People don't share honestly when they feel they might be judged**. If a group member believes that someone in the group might judge their behavior or "correct" their way of thinking, he or she will be less likely to honestly share their true thoughts and experiences. They will either leave the group entirely or else share only on a superficial basis.

- **In a safe environment, people will often seek input from other caring people**. Once a person feels loved and accepted, he or she will often solicit input from others on issues with which they are struggling. When such advice or input is solicited, it should be given in the spirit of one struggler sharing his or her perspective with another struggler, and not in a patronizing manner as one who "knows it all" to one who needs instruction. It should be done in the spirit of "speaking the truth in love" (Eph. 4:15), and mindful of how difficult it is sometimes to ask for such input. If a person knows he or she might receive input critical of their own behavior, asking for it is an act of bravery. It is saying that to him or her, growing in Christ is too important to let pride and sensitivity hold them back. An old saying asks for the grace to "see ourselves as others see us." Such does indeed take a lot of grace.

- **Each group member needs to focus primarily on his or her own spiritual growth needs**. People who do not want to deal with their own issues or face hard changes will try anything to avoid doing so, and one of the things they often try is to focus on what other people need to change or learn, instead of what they themselves need to change or learn. Each of us has all he or she can handle working on our own issues, and that is the primary task God places before us.

- **Acceptance helps a person reach for his or her best**. We look to the example of our God and Father who loved us "while we were still sinners" (Rom. 5:8.) His love and acceptance is not to make us complacent about where we are. Rather it takes away the pressure of rejection, helping us to be the person He created us to be. Acceptance helps us to see that it is safe to see ourselves as we really are, and when it is safe to do that, we can also see for ourselves (often without the interference or direction of someone else) where we can improve.

- **Doctrinal correction is best done by those commissioned to the task**. Pastors and teachers are the ones called, commissioned and trained to teach doctrine, and they are the ones to do the difficult task of correcting people in regard to doctrine. In the story we will look at today, it is possible that Priscilla and Aquila were left by Paul in Ephesus to help teach the church there, at least the record of the correction of Apollos is positive.

ICEBREAKER
Connect with your Group | **15 Min.**

LEADER

Remember to assign a different member of the group each week to lead this Icebreaker. In leading the Icebreaker it is important to go around in the circle and have each person share in turn.

To help your group members get acquainted, have each person take turns answering all three of the Icebreaker questions.

In his efforts to share the gospel with as many persons as possible, Paul did a great deal of traveling. Some people would think of that as a "perk" of the job, and some would think of it as a definite drawback. How do you feel about traveling? Share your own feelings about life on the road by answering the following questions.

1. What would you say was the most interesting place where you have traveled? What did you especially like about being there?

2. Who do you remember meeting during your travels who you wished you could have spent more time with?

3. What is the hardest thing about traveling for you?
   - Saying good-bye to the people I meet.
   - Packing and unpacking all the time.
   - Paying all that money!
   - Not being able to sleep in my own bed.
   - Missing my normal routines.
   - Knowing it has to end.
   - other _____.

BIBLE STUDY
Read Scripture and Discuss | **30 Min.**

LEADER

Select a person from your group to read the following passages from Acts 18: 18-28.

Paul was perhaps the best-known traveling Christian church planter of all time. However, he did not do the work he did on his own. There were others like him whom many of us do not know as well. The following is a section of Acts dealing with three of them, Apollos and a husband-wife team, Priscilla and Aquila. Their work reminds us that when we work for the Lord, we can do important things without ever getting the "headlines." Apollos, who was a very learned man, especially did some important work in Corinth. However, before he went there, Priscilla and Aquila found they had some things that they had learned about the Christian faith that they needed to share with Apollos. Some people believe they already know it all, and for that reason don't take such instruction very well. Apparently, however, such was not the case with Apollos. Filled with even more understanding he went on to a vital preaching and teaching ministry in Greece. As you read the passage and answer the questions that follow, think of how you react to being instructed or admonished by others.

[18] So Paul, having stayed on for many days, said good-bye to the brothers and sailed away to Syria. Priscilla and Aquila were with him. He shaved his head at Cenchreae, because he had taken a vow. [19] When they reached Ephesus he left them there, but he himself entered the synagogue and engaged in discussion with the Jews. [20] And though they asked him to stay for a longer time, he declined, [21] but said good-bye and stated, "I'll come back to you again, if God wills." Then he set sail from Ephesus.

[22] On landing at Caesarea, he went up and greeted the church, and went down to Antioch. [23] He set out, traveling through one place after another in the Galatian territory and Phrygia, strengthening all the disciples.

[24] A Jew named Apollos, a native Alexandrian, an eloquent man who was powerful in the Scriptures, arrived in Ephesus. [25] This man had been instructed in the way of the Lord; and being fervent in spirit, he spoke and taught the things about Jesus accurately, although he knew only John's baptism. [26] He began to speak boldly in the synagogue. After Priscilla and Aquila heard him, they took him home and explained the way of God to him more accurately. [27] When he wanted to cross over to Achaia, the brothers wrote to the disciples urging them to welcome him. After he arrived, he greatly helped those who had believed through grace. [28] For he vigorously refuted the Jews in public, demonstrating through the Scriptures that Jesus is the Messiah.

Acts 18:18-28

 | # QUESTIONS FOR INTERACTION

LEADER

Divide the group into subgroups of three to six persons each, and assign someone to lead each subgroup.

Refer to the Summary and Study Notes at the end of this section as needed. If 30 minutes is not enough time to answer all of the questions in this section, conclude the Bible Study by answering questions 6 and 7.

1. What is the most unusual reason you have ever had for cutting your hair?
   - getting a "buzz cut" on a dare
   - to enter the armed forces
   - getting a strange haircut as part of an initiation
   - getting a buzz cut or carving letters in my hair to go to a sporting event
   - cutting my hair to look like a celebrity
   - cutting my hair for a role in a play
   - getting a haircut I didn't like to please my parents
   - cutting my hair to get rid of lice
   - getting a buzz cut to identify with a cancer victim receiving radiation treatment
   - other _____.

2. Why does Paul get his hair cut (see Notes v. 18)? What does it say to you about him that he did this?

3. What does Paul do while traveling through Galatia and Phrygia? What specifically do you think this entailed?

4. What did Priscilla and Aquila feel the need to talk to Apollos about? Why was it so important for them to "explain the way of God more accurately to him" in this area of Christian faith?

5. Had you been Apollos, how would you have reacted to Priscilla and Aquila's desire to "explain the way of God more accurately" to you?
   • with irritation – "What makes you such know-it-alls?"
   • with embarrassment – "Why didn't someone tell me this before?"
   • with gratitude – "This is really important to know!"
   • with retaliation – "Okay, now let me tell you something YOU don't know!"
   • other _____

6. If a Christian brother or sister is to effectively talk to you about something they feel you need to know or to do differently, how should they do it? Which of the following is most important?
   • They should be someone I know is willing to receive such instruction themselves.
   • They should affirm what I am doing well first.
   • They should do it in a non-didactic way: "Have you ever considered...?" and not "This is the way it is!"
   • They shouldn't do it unless they are commissioned by the church to do it.
   • They should seek the Holy Spirit's guidance about what to say.
   • I prefer someone to just explore the questions with me rather than trying to give me the answers.
   • other _____

7. What do you need a "Priscilla" or an "Aquila" to explain to you more accurately in relation to the "way of God"?

GOING DEEPER: *If your group has time and/or wants a challenge, go on to these questions.*

8. How could you deal with a person who always wanted to "correct" everyone else but never was willing to examine his or her own life?

9. As a group leader how would you deal with a group member whom you felt was pushing a view of Christian faith that you believe is wrong or unbiblical?

CARING TIME Apply the Lesson & Pray for One another | 15 Min.

***LEADER

Use this time to develop and express your concern for each other as group members by praying for one another. Bring the group back together and begin the Caring Time by sharing responses to all three questions. In this session, encourage everyone to pray at will before you close. First have group members answer the following questions.

1. Take time to pray for God's direction on the issues brought up in question 7 above.

2. Has anything that we have discussed today or in previous sessions made you anxious about your ability to be a small-group leader? Pray for God's strength and direction in relation to any such anxiety.

3. What are you facing in the coming week that you could use some support or direction with?

NEXT WEEK

Today we looked at what it means to admonish each other, and the importance of doing this in the proper spirit. Next week we will deal with a related issue, the matter of controversy in the group. What happens when there are sharp divisions in a group that you are seeking to help towards a closer fellowship? To consider this issue we will look at how the early church dealt with a controversy in Acts 15. As always, make sure that you read the small Introduction section at the beginning of next week's session prior to the session.

Summary: What the church was bringing in the book of Acts may be described as nothing less than a quiet revolution. Perhaps the most visible aspect of that revolution was the role of women in Jewish society. Previous to Jesus, women were not allowed to study Scripture and were not supposed to follow a rabbi. Whatever spiritual knowledge they attained was to be gleaned from their husbands or the other men in their life. But women became an important part of Jesus' following (see for example Luke 8:1-3.) In this story, the name of Priscilla is listed ahead of her husband Aquila. That is virtually unprecedented and indicates that she was considered an important part of their ministry. Romans 16:3-4 tells us that she and her husband risked their lives for Paul.

For the most part, Christianity took root and grew among the uneducated poor and working people – fishermen, those with disabilities, lepers, and prostitutes. But with Apollos, the faith got a foothold among the intelligentsia of the era. He was from Alexandria, a major intellectual and cultural center of the day. In fact Ptolemy of Greece wanted Alexandria to be the intellectual capital of the world. All of this is to say that Apollos may have been an important link to the spreading of the gospel to the most educated people of the day.

Our passage says that Apollos went to Achaia, another name for Greece. Corinth was a city where he apparently had a great deal of influence.

18:18 Priscilla and Aquila were with him. It is significant here that Priscilla's name is listed first here ahead of her husband. This was hardly ever done, and probably indicates that Priscilla was an influential person. Cenchreae. A port city near Corinth (see Rom. 16:1). **he had taken a vow**. Pious Jews would take vows, based on the pattern of the Nazarites (Num. 6:1-21), as an indication of their devotion to God. Since the cutting of one's hair indicated the termination of the vow, Paul may have made a vow of dedication to God for as long as he was in Corinth in gratefulness to God's promise of protection (v. 10). While normally vows would be terminated by shaving one's head and offering a sacrifice in the Temple at Jerusalem, people far from

the city could shave their heads where they were and carry the trimmings to the Temple to be presented along with a sacrifice at that time. Luke may have included this incident as evidence that Paul did not abandon the traditions of his people.

18:19-21 The positive response to Paul among the Jews at Ephesus sets the stage for his return to that city in 19:1. Priscilla and Aquila stayed on at Ephesus and established the new church there.

18:22-23 Because of his vow, Paul undoubtedly went to Jerusalem to offer a thank offering. Then he proceeded to Antioch, the church that had spawned his missionary work in the first place (13:1-3). He may have stayed there until the spring (A.D. 52 or 53) when traveling would again be possible. From there he visited the churches throughout the area where he had established churches on his first trip (13:13-14:20). **strengthening all the disciples**. Paul was not the kind of evangelist who was only interested in saving souls in order to "put notches on his spiritual belt." He was also very careful to come back to them to nurture them along the way. (See also 14:21-22.)

18:24-28 During Paul's journey, Apollos visited Ephesus. While Apollos is a minor figure in Acts (nothing more is said of him after 19:1), he was a significant figure in the church at Corinth and became a valued associate of Paul's (1 Cor. 1:12; 3:4-23; 16:12; perhaps 2 Cor. 8:22). Some modern scholars, following Luther, wonder if Apollos might have authored Hebrews. This incident, as well as that in 19:1-7, shows that Acts records only a small part of the story of how the gospel was spread throughout the known world. While unfortunately their stories are not recorded, the other apostles, as well as many unknown believers, played important roles in spreading the story of Jesus far beyond Judea.

18:24 a native Alexandrian. Alexandria was a major cultural center on the northern coast of Egypt. Jews from this area were present at Pentecost and undoubtedly carried the message back home (2:10).

18:25-26 While Apollos was an earnest, articulate believer in Jesus, he had not received the whole story of the gospel. Just what he was lacking is unclear, but, as the story in 19:1-7 indicates, he may have not heard of the coming of the Spir-

it promised to those who are baptized in the name of Jesus. **Priscilla and Aquila**. Once again Priscilla's name is mentioned first. Here it is especially significant because of the instruction of an educated man. That her husband was with her probably made this more socially acceptable, but it appears she was an active part of the instruction. Apollos, in turn, must have been a remarkably progressive man to humbly receive instruction from a couple during such an era as this. **the way of God**. The various sermons in Acts record what Luke considered essential for the understanding of "the way".

18:27-28 Whether the church at Ephesus encouraged Apollos to go to Corinth, or if they encouraged the Corinthians to receive Apollos is uncertain from the Greek, and either is possible. Because of Apollos' zeal, scriptural understanding, classical education and his ability to communicate, they may have felt he would be perfect for the sophisticated, worldly atmosphere at Corinth. At a later date Paul likewise encouraged Apollos to return to Corinth, but he refused to do so (1 Cor. 16:12), perhaps because he wanted nothing to do with the faction in the Corinthian church that favored him over Paul. **he greatly helped those who had believed through grace**. Lit. "he contributed much to the ones having believed through grace." Two readings are possible. The HCSB lays the emphasis on God's grace to the Corinthians which caused them to believe. It can also be translated as "he contributed much through grace to the believers" putting the emphasis on Apollos' ability as a gift from God useful for helping the believers.

SESSION 6

DEALING WITH CONTROVERSY

SCRIPTURE: ACTS 15:1-21

LAST WEEK

Last week we looked at what it means to admonish each other, and the importance of doing this in the proper spirit. This week we will deal with a related issue, the matter of controversy in the group. What happens when there are sharp divisions in a group that you are seeking to help towards a closer fellowship? To consider this issue we will look at how the early church dealt with a controversy in Acts 15.

Every group that includes human beings will also include some conflict and controversy. It's simply the nature of who we are as people. The important thing for a small-group leader to do is to make sure that such conflict is handled wisely when it comes. Here are some guidelines to help in that process:

- **Make sure everyone present is included**. A person who does not feel included in a group is more likely to instigate a conflict situation. People are included through the process of having everyone respond to the Icebreaker and personal sharing questions. This allows everyone to tell his or her story. Be careful to keep anyone from dominating the conversation. Some people, once they start telling their story, don't want to stop. This keeps others from sharing. When someone goes on too long, the leader needs to say something like, "You have told us some very interesting things. But in order to end on time we need to go on to someone else. (Next person), would you share on our question now?" Including everyone also means making sure that "the playing field is level." The playing field is level when people are sharing on their own story, because we are all experts on our own story. When we are talking about academic issues related to Bible knowledge, the playing field is not level, because some of us have more Bible knowledge than others. A lack of Bible knowledge makes some feel excluded. In Serendipity material we have what is called "the option play." This means that if a new person joins your group, you should assume that they don't know a lot about the Bible. You should then make sure that a higher percentage of the questions are personally-oriented. Do all of the Icebreaker questions instead of just one or two. Skip some of the more knowledge-oriented questions (generally questions 2-5 or 2-6) and focus more on the personally-oriented Bible study questions (question 1 and either 6-7 or 7-8.)

- **Focus on self-revelation**. We covered some of this above. But it is important to note that the more you focus on knowledge or academic questions, the more room there is for conflict and controversy. There are different ways of interpreting many scriptural teachings, and many different implications people make for lifestyle and political issues. These can be handled in a mature group that has learned to love each other, but might put too much pressure on a new group of people with diverse opinions. When we focus on our stories and apply Scripture to our own personal lives, there is less room for conflict and controversy.

- **Accept the nature of the church**. The church is a diverse body (see 1 Cor. 12). The church includes many different cultures, many different kinds of personalities and many different perspectives. We can fight this, trying to force everyone in the church to be more like us, but it will be a discouraging, losing battle. It has been said that if we all think the same way, then only one of us is necessary. In the church, ALL of us are necessary.

- **Call in the Holy Spirit**. It is the Spirit that makes us one (1 Cor. 12:13.) When conflict occurs, it is especially important to call upon the Holy Spirit to come into your group and bind you together as one. Relying exclusively on our own wisdom is divisive.

 **ICEBREAKER** Connect with your Group | **15 Min.**

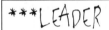 ***LEADER

Once again assign a member of the group to lead this Icebreaker. If there is someone in the group who has not done so yet, he or she should be chosen. In leading the Icebreaker it is important to go around in the circle and have each person share in turn.

In the story we will be looking at this week, the church had a kind of "family meeting" to resolve a dispute that had arisen in the fellowship. Principally it dealt with whether Gentiles who converted to the Christian faith needed to obey established Jewish rules like having their males all circumcised. This reminds us that all families have conflicts that they need to resolve. How about the family in which you were raised? Share some of your own history of family rules by answering the following questions.

1. When you were a teenager, when do you remember something you did prompting a "family meeting"? How was the situation resolved?

2. When you were a teen, what family rule were you most likely to challenge?

3. If you could make just four rules to govern how families should operate, what would those rules be?

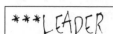

Sometimes we think that since the church is a Christian organization, it shouldn't have any conflicts. However, conflict has been part of the church right from the beginning. In the following story we read of a rather serious conflict they had over whether Gentiles should obey long-established Jewish rules and traditions like circumcision. As we look at this story we can see that, while churches will always have such conflicts, it is how such conflicts are resolved that is most important. Here the conflict is resolved by listening to each other and arriving at a win-win situation. This provides a good example for our churches and small groups as well. As you read this story and answer the questions that follow, explore what it says to you about conflict resolution.

Narrator: [1] Some men came down from Judea and began to teach the brothers:

Traditionalists: "Unless you are circumcised according to the custom prescribed by Moses, you cannot be saved!"

Narrator: [2] But after Paul and Barnabas had engaged them in serious argument and debate, they arranged for Paul and Barnabas and some others of them to go up to the apostles and elders in Jerusalem concerning this controversy. [3] When they had been sent on their way by the church, they passed through both Phoenicia and Samaria, explaining in detail the conversion of the Gentiles, and they created great joy among all the brothers.

[4] When they arrived at Jerusalem, they were welcomed by the church, the apostles, and the elders, and they reported all that God had done with them. [5] But some of the believers from the party of the Pharisees stood up and said,

Traditionalists: "It is necessary to circumcise them and to command them to keep the law of Moses!"

Narrator: [6] Then the apostles and the elders assembled to consider this matter. [7] After there had been much debate, Peter stood up and said to them:

Peter: "Brothers, you are aware that in the early days God made a choice among you, that by my mouth the Gentiles would hear the gospel message and believe. [8] And God, who knows the heart, testified to them by giving the Holy Spirit, just as He also did to us. [9] He made no distinction between us and them, cleansing their hearts by faith. [10] Why, then, are you now testing God by putting on the disciples' necks a yoke that neither our forefathers nor we have been able to bear? [11] On the contrary, we believe we are saved through the grace of the Lord Jesus, in the same way they are."

Narrator: [12] Then the whole assembly fell silent and listened to Barnabas and Paul describing all the signs and wonders God had done through them among the Gentiles. [13] After they stopped speaking, James responded:

James: "Brothers, listen to me! [14] Simeon has reported how God first intervened to take from the Gentiles a people for His name. [15] And the words of the prophets agree with this, as it is written:
> [16] After these things I will return and will rebuild David's tent, which has fallen down.I will rebuild its ruins and will set it up again,

> [17] so that those who are left of mankind may seek the Lord—even all the Gentiles who are called by My name, says the Lord who does these things,

> [18] which have been known from long ago.

[19] Therefore, in my judgment, we should not cause difficulties for those who turn to God from among the Gentiles, [20] but instead we should write to them to abstain from things polluted by idols, from sexual immorality, from eating anything that has been strangled, and from blood. [21] For since ancient times, Moses has had in every city those who proclaim him, and he is read aloud in the synagogues every Sabbath day."

Acts 15:1-21

QUESTIONS FOR INTERACTION

***LEADER

Divide the group into subgroups of
three to six persons each, and assign
someone to lead each subgroup. It is
best to assign people who did not have
the chance to lead last week.

The opening question in this study is a
lighter question relating the story to
one's own personal experience. Go
around and have each person share on
this question in turn. Questions numbered 2 to 6 relate to understanding
the content of the passage. Persons
should be encouraged to respond to
these questions at will. Questions
numbered 7 and 8 help group members
apply the text to their own personal
lives, and once again on these the
leader should have each person share
on the question in turn.

Refer to the Summary and Study Notes
at the end of this section as needed. If
30 minutes is not enough time to
answer all of the questions in this section, conclude the Bible Study by
answering questions 7 and 8.

1. How does the meeting in this passage compare with church meetings that you have been familiar with?
   - At least they didn't have to argue about whether to sing hymns or praise songs!
   - This meeting got right to the issue – ours seem to skirt the issues
   - People seemed to listen to each other better then.
   - Didn't women have any opinions back then?
   - They seemed to have stronger leaders.
   - other _____.

2. What do you think the motivation was for those who came from Judea to raise this issue?
   - They thought they were standing up for "good old fashion values".
   - They didn't want anyone else getting off without doing something they had to do.
   - They really didn't like Gentiles.
   - They sincerely believed the Gentiles needed this for salvation.
   - other _____.

3. How did Paul and Barnabas respond to the challenge of the men from Judea? Would you have done anything differently?

4. According to what Peter says, in what ways were the Gentiles no different than the Jews (see verses 8-9)? Why does he make this point (see verses 10-11)?

5. How does the assembly respond to what Paul and Barnabas had to share about their work among the Gentiles? Why was it important for Paul and Barnabas to share this with them? Why was it important that the assembly listened silently?

6. Who makes the final decision about what is to be done in regard to this dispute? What does the decision offer to the Jewish traditionalists, and what does it offer to Paul's missionary team evangelizing the Gentiles?

7. Listening was an important part of this resolution (verses 12-13). How hard is it for you to listen while a controversial matter is being discussed?
   - very hard – I want to get my argument in!
   - moderately hard – some points get through to me

- moderately easy — I hear most of the points that are made
- very easy — I love a debate and I always learn a lot.
- difficult — I don't like contention.

8. What is the most important thing you personally feel you need to learn from the way this conflict in the early church was handled?
   - I need to talk directly to the authorities in question (vv. 2-3)
   - I myself should be less legalistic (vv. 10-11)
   - I need to listen better (vv. 12-13)
   - I need to know what the Scripture says on the conflict in question (vv. 16-18)
   - I need to seek a win-win solution (vv. 19-20)
   - other _____.

9. When GOING DEEPER: *If your group has time and/or wants a challenge, go on to these questions.*

   should a person "bend a little" in a church conflict, and when should one stand firm on principle? Which happened in this situation, and what does that say to you?

10. In what way does the church today sometimes "cause difficulties for those who turn to God" from other than a church-related background? What can we learn from this story about this problem?

CARING TIME *Apply the Lesson & Pray for One another* **15 Min.**

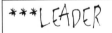

***LEADER

Bring the group back together and begin the Caring Time by sharing responses to all three questions. In this session, encourage group members to pray at will before you close. First have group members answer the following questions.

1. How do you feel this group is doing in listening to each other? Who in the group do you feel has done a particularly good job of listening to you? Take time to thank God for the listening that has been done.

2. What controversy in your church do you feel the need to pray for right now? (Take care not to debate the different sides right now — rather pray for a resolution in the spirit of what happened in our story).

3. Pray for the shortcomings in conflict-resolution skills that people mentioned in question #8.

NEXT WEEK

Today we looked at how a controversy in the early church was handled, and what we might learn from the process they went through. Next week we will consider the centrality of prayer, especially as it relates to the life of a small-group. We will look at how the disciples prayed in Acts 12:1-17, and we will learn from what they did wrong as well as what they did right. As always, make sure that you read the small Introduction section at the beginning of next week's session prior to the session.

NOTES ON ACTS 15:1-21

Summary: Right in the middle of Luke's account is this record of the council in Jerusalem which met to discuss the status of Gentiles in the church. The controversy surrounding circumcision stirred up such a debate that the church felt it necessary to call together the recognized leaders from Jerusalem and Antioch to settle the issue. This is considered to be the first Church Council. This critical meeting of the church marked its first self-conscious departure from orthodox Judaism. Had the council decided to support the claims of the Jewish believers, Christianity would have remained only another sect within Judaism.

15:1 down from Judea. Judea would have been the center of the part of the church that believed it necessary for even Christians to maintain Jewish tradition. Some people from this group went to Antioch, an early center of the Gentile church.

15:2 to go up to the apostles and elders in Jerusalem. The authority structure of the church seems fairly simple at this point. The apostles are the original core of Jesus disciples, and the elders are those who had leadership status by virtue of both age and respect in the community. It would appear that the mother church in Jerusalem, perhaps because of the apostles who were there, had some authority over the rest of the church.

15:5 the believers from the party of the Pharisees. The resistance to allowing Gentiles into the church originated with Jewish Christians who had formerly been Pharisees. This small but influential sect was widely respected for its adherence to the Law and traditions. Their concern arose from a genuine desire to insure that God's honor was not violated through disregard of his law. To them, the offer of the gospel apart from the law was inconceivable since for centuries their people had been taught to look to the law to discern God's will. Paul's ministry seemed like a slap in Israel's face - an unthinkable rejection of all the covenant responsibilities of God's chosen people.

15:7-8 As part of the discussion, Peter recounts his experience with Cornelius which may have occurred 10 or more years earlier (10:1-11:18). The fact that Cornelius experienced the presence of the Spirit in the same way the disciples did was proof to him that God accepted the Gentiles quite apart from the practice of Jewish law.

15:9-11 It is by faith in Jesus that one is made pure by God. The fact that it has to be that way is made plain by the fact that neither Israel as a nation nor any Jew as an individual ever managed to live up to all the demands of the law. This affirmation of God's intent to save Gentiles through faith in Jesus is Peter's last statement in Acts.

15:12 Peter's recounting of his experience with Cornelius prepared the church to hear the first-hand reports of the work of Barnabas and Paul (see 14:3).

15:13-21 James (the brother of Jesus) was the leader of the Jerusalem church and perhaps of the church as a whole, and the ultimate decision as to the position of the Jerusalem church was his to make. Since in Galatians 2:11-13 James appears to have represented those who believed that Gentiles could not be considered equal members of the church with Jews, it may be that this council was the turning point when he realized the scope of Jesus' mission. James' affirmation of God's plan to save all types of people through faith in Jesus is his last statement in Acts as well.

15:15 the words of the prophets. James' quote is primarily rooted in the Septuagint version of Amos 9:11-12. The OT books of Hosea -Malachi were contained on a single scroll. To quote one was to assume the support of the others.

15:16-18 The original context of the prophecy was the anticipation of the destruction of Israel (722 B.C.) after which God would one day return the nation to its former glory as in David's day. James sees that the way God is rebuilding "David's ...tent" (a symbol of God's presence with Israel) is by establishing His church, made up of all types of people who seek God. The differences between the Septuagint version quoted here and what is found in our OT are a result of adding a "d" to the Hebrew word yiresu (possessing) to obtain yirdresu (seeking), and a dispute about whether the Hebrew word dm should be vocalized as Edom (the name of a country south of Israel) or as adam (the Hebrew word for humanity). In either case, the point is that God's new people will include Gentiles as well as Jews.

15:19-21 we should write to them to abstain from...blood. These considerations sum up the law in Leviticus 17-28 that applied to Israel and all foreigners who lived within her borders. **things polluted by idols**. In Gentile areas meat was sold only after the animal had been sacrificed as part of a worship service to an idol. The eating of such food was later to be a source of controversy between Jewish and Gentile believers in Rome (Rom. 14:1:8) and Corinth (1 Cor. 8). **sexual immorality**. This may be related to "the pollution of idols" since idolatry sometimes involved ritual sexual immorality (1 Cor. 6:12-20). **from eating anything that has been strangled, and from blood**. Jews were forbidden to eat meat that had any blood in it (Lev. 17:10,13): Gentiles would make the sharing of meals with Jewish believers easier if they would respect this tradition.

SESSION 7

THE CENTRALITY OF PRAYER

SCRIPTURE: Acts 12:1-17

Last week we looked at how the controversy over Gentiles and circumcision was handled in the early church, and we discovered what we could learn from the process they went through. This week we will consider the centrality of prayer, especially as it relates to the life of a small-group. We will look at how the disciples prayed in Acts 12:1-17, and we will learn from what they did wrong as well as what they did right.

There are many different attitudes in the church concerning what prayer is and what it does. Here are some typical ones:

- **Prayer is a traditional ritual** – For those who see prayer this way, it is simply what one does in certain worship services and at ritually proscribed times. For such persons, prayer should be done by a religious authority, who is trained in the "right" words to use. Such prayer is seldom viewed as having much power – it is just the right thing to do.

- **Prayer is a form of magic** – It is how religious people get what they want and control their world. If we are a child who prays for a bike for Christmas, our prayer should deliver a bike. If we pray for that promotion we are wanting, the promotion should be ours. If we pray that our loved one will live, the next day or even the next moment they should be dramatically better. In this view, what God wants in not what matters, it's what we want. God's job is to deliver what we want. But this is the exact opposite of what the Bible talks about when it calls us to faith. Faith means submission to God's control, not using God's power to maintain our own control.

- **Prayer is just sharing our feelings with God** – In this view prayer is similar to talking to any other loved one. We tell Him what is going on in our life and what we feel about it. We express our love for Him, and we seek His advice or direction. There is much truth in this perspective. However, one must also note that the Bible does call us not only to share our thoughts and feelings, but to ask God for what we need (Matt. 7:7-11.)

Prayer, then means both sharing our thoughts and feelings with God, as well as taking our needs to Him. When we take our needs to Him, we must acknowledge that He is the one who remains in control, not us. But we must also believe that God's power is such that all things are possible, and even when what we request seems unlikely or even impossible, God can do it.

In terms of what we pray for in a small group, the needs of members are central. This is not to say that praying for world peace or a solution to homelessness is not important. However, in this context, focusing on such larger concerns depersonalizes the sessions. It's easier to raise a concern for homelessness than it is to admit that you personally need prayer for a struggle you have with a rebellious teenager or an ailing marriage. Focusing on the needs of members is an essential part of building the group as a group where people care for each other.

There is one area, however, where group prayer focuses regularly beyond the group. This is in the prayer for the "empty chair." Each week the group circle should include an empty chair, reminding group members that there are other persons out there in the world who need the caring community of the group. It is the mission of the group each week to fill that empty chair. This means taking time to pray for God to bring someone into your group to fill that chair. In this way the group helps the kingdom of God to grow one person at a time.

ICEBREAKER   *Connect with your Group* | **15 Min.**

When the church first came into being it was quickly attacked by the Enemy. Some died a martyr's death, some were imprisoned and some were merely harassed. Most of us have not had these things happen to us, at least to that extent. However, most of us do know what it is like to feel like we are under attack. What has been your experience with this? Share your own experience with feeling like you were under attack by answering the following questions.

1. When you were a child or adolescent who or what did you feel most "under attack" from?
   - A sibling – he/she never left me alone.
   - My parents – they were on my back all of the time.
   - A school bully – I didn't know how to defend myself.
   - My own self – I was relentlessly self-critical.
   - A rival – he/she was always gossiping about me or giving me a hard time.
   - I don't remember ever feeling "under attack."
   - other _____

2. In what area of your life do you most feel "under attack" right now?
   - My professional life – nothing I do seems good enough.
   - My spiritual life – Satan is trying to bring me down.
   - My role as a parent – everyone thinks he or she can do it better than I do.

- My integrity as a person – I feel judged by a lot of people.
- other _____

3. When you feel "under attack", what are you most likely to do?
   - return fire
   - run for cover
   - see if I can negotiate a cease-fire
   - wave a white flag
   - other _____

 BIBLE STUDY *Read Scripture and Discuss* | **30 Min.**

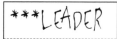

Select a person from
your group to read the
following passage from
Acts 12:1-17.

The history of the early church is a history of facing persecution. It started with the martyr death of Stephen (Acts 7:54 – 8:3) and the subsequent persecution led by Saul of Tarsus, and after a short reprieve was picked up again here under King Herod Agrippa. This persecution would continue sporadically until the fourth century. During all that time the church's manner of defending itself was not through physical power or retaliation, but through the power of prayer and a bold witness. In this story the disciples immediately turn to prayer on behalf of Peter, but they don't yet seem to trust its power. When their prayers result in Peter's release, they cannot believe what has happened. This story speaks volumes to us about a proper attitude in prayer. As you read the story, think of your own expectations regarding the power of prayer, and consider what God may be saying to you about the role of prayer in making a difference in our world.

12 About that time King Herod cruelly attacked some who belonged to the church, [2] and he killed James, John's brother, with the sword. [3] When he saw that it pleased the Jews, he proceeded to arrest Peter too, during the days of Unleavened Bread. [4] After the arrest, he put him in prison and assigned four squads of four soldiers each to guard him, intending to bring him out to the people after the Passover. [5] So Peter was kept in prison, but prayer was being made earnestly to God for him by the church.

[6] On the night before Herod was to bring him out for execution, Peter was sleeping between two soldiers, bound with two chains, while the sentries in front of the door guarded the prison. [7] Suddenly an angel of the Lord appeared, and a light shone in the cell. Striking Peter on the side, he woke him up and said, "Quick, get up!" Then the chains fell off his wrists. [8] "Get dressed," the angel told him, "and put on your sandals." And he did so. "Wrap your cloak around you," he told him, "and follow me." [9] So he went out and followed, and he did not know that what took place through the angel was real, but thought he was seeing a vision. [10] After they passed the first and second guard posts, they came to the iron gate that leads into the city,

which opened to them by itself. They went outside and passed one street, and immediately the angel left him.

¹¹ Then Peter came to himself and said, "Now I know for certain that the Lord has sent His angel and rescued me from Herod's grasp and from all that the Jewish people expected." ¹² When he realized this, he went to the house of Mary, the mother of John Mark, where many had assembled and were praying. ¹³ He knocked at the door in the gateway, and a servant named Rhoda came to answer. ¹⁴ She recognized Peter's voice, and because of her joy she did not open the gate, but ran in and announced that Peter was standing at the gateway.

¹⁵ "You're crazy!" they told her. But she kept insisting that it was true. Then they said, "It's his angel!" ¹⁶ Peter, however, kept on knocking, and when they opened the door and saw him, they were astounded.

¹⁷ Motioning to them with his hand to be silent, he explained to them how the Lord had brought him out of the prison. "Report these things to James and the brothers," he said. Then he departed and went to a different place.

Acts 12:1-17

 ## QUESTIONS FOR INTERACTION

***LEADER

Divide the group into subgroups of three to six persons each, and assign someone to lead each subgroup. It is best to assign people who did not have the chance to lead last week.

Refer to the Summary and Study Notes at the end of this section as needed. If 30 minutes is not enough time to answer all of the questions in this section, conclude the Bible Study by answering questions 6 and 7.

1. What experience have you had that you found yourself at odds with civil authority? Where you afraid of going to jail?

2. How many soldiers does Herod assign to guard Peter? Why does he go to such lengths to provide this security (see Notes on verses 4 and 7)?

3. Why do you think it took Peter so long to realize that he was being rescued by an angel of God?
   - He had been sleeping and thought it was all a dream.
   - It's just not what you expect to happen.
   - Angels are often mistaken for men.
   - other _____

4. Why were the disciples so slow to believe that Peter was at the door, even though they had been praying for his release?

5. How do you think this miraculous escape from prison affected the prayer life of the Christians in Jerusalem?

6. What are you praying for right now that you would be as surprised about if it were answered favorably as these disciples were?

7. What can you as a Christian small group leader do to affirm the power of prayer to the members of the group you will be leading?

 GOING DEEPER: *If your group has time and/or wants a challenge, go on to this question.*

8. What does it say to you that James was killed while Peter was freed, even though the church probably prayed for both?

9. What is the bigger danger for Christians — expecting prayer to always result in miraculous intervention, or expecting prayer to have little or no effect?

CARING TIME *Apply the Lesson & Pray for One another* | 15 Min.

1. What would you like this group to be in prayer for in relation to the challenges you expect to be facing as a small-group leader?

2. How can this group be in prayer for you in relation to the concern you mentioned in question 6 above?

3. What God–sized challenge is your church facing that needs the power of prayer right now?

This week we considered the centrality of prayer, especially as it relates to the life of a small-group. We did this by looking at the story of Peter's release from prison and the role prayer played in that release. Next week in our final session we will examine the need for a small group to take on the mission of multiplying itself. This keeps a group from becoming an ingrown clique and it helps us be part of the growth of the kingdom of God.

NOTES ON ACTS 12:1-17

Summary: While Saul, now called Paul, was no longer persecuting the church, that did not mean that persecution of the church was over. The agency of persecution shifts in the following story from zealous Pharisees to the Rome-appointed king, Herod Agrippa. He finds that having James the son of Zebedee killed is a popular move among the Jewish leaders, and therefore he also has Peter arrested. He plans to railroad him through a trial and have him executed also, but God intervenes by sending His angel to deliver Peter from prison. The church, which has been praying for just such a deliverance, does not believe at first that it has really happened. But when they see Peter actually standing at the gate of the house where they are holding their prayer meeting, their attitude is changed.

12:1 King Herod. This is Herod Agrippa I, the grandson of Herod the Great, who ruled when Jesus was born, and the nephew of Herod Antipas who governed Galilee during Jesus' ministry. Herod Agippa I was popular with the Jews; some even wondered if he might be the Messiah who would free them from Rome. To further cultivate this popularity, he resumed the persecution of the church which had ceased upon Paul's conversion (9:31). Since Herod died in A.D. 44, this story precedes the visit of Paul and Barnabas to Jerusalem.

12:2 James, John's brother. James and John were the sons of Zebedee. When their mother asked for prominent places for them in the kingdom, Jesus asked if they were able to drink from the cup He was going to drink. This meant to share His same fate of suffering. James here is the first of the original twelve to share Christ's suffering through martyrdom (Judas died at his own hand, and not out of the martyrdom of faith).

12:4 four squads of four soldiers each. Each squad would be on watch for six hours in order to watch through a 24-

hour period. **after the Passover**. It would have been considered sacrilegious to try a person or execute them during the Passover.

12:7 a light shone. Similarities between this story and other escape stories circulating in the first century have led some commentators to assume that supernatural overtones were added to an account of how Peter was released with the help of a sympathetic insider. However, this fails to account for how the security measures used to imprison Peter could have been circumvented. Peter was constantly guarded by four soldiers on six hour shifts (vv.4,6) . Two soldiers were in the cell with Peter chained to their wrists, while the other two stood guard at the door. Such intense security measures may have been implemented precisely to prevent any such "unexplainable" release such as happened when the Sanhedrin had imprisoned him earlier (5:19-41). The description of the light, a common symbol of divine glory, underscores that this was a miraculous intervention of God.

12:8-10 In a trance-like state, Peter was led past the prison's guard and through the main door of the prison.

12:11 the Lord...rescued me from Herod's grasp. In Acts, there is no predictable pattern of how God will work. While Peter was released from prison, James, for whom the church undoubtedly prayed just as earnestly,   was killed. Dorcas, a kindly but relatively insignificant woman (9:36-43), is raised from the dead while a bold, courageous man like Stephen is not. Even in this account, Peter, although so miraculously protected by God, decides he should go into hiding lest Herod catch him again (v. 17). The answer to why these things should be so is not given. It is not a matter of Peter being more deserving, or moral, or having more faith than James. The mystery is only known in the secret counsel of God who works all things according to His will: the call to the church is to be faithful and take responsible action whether or not God chooses to act in a miraculous way.

12:12 Mary, the mother of John Mark This is the Mark who later wrote the Gospel bearing that name (see v.25; 13:5).

12:13-17 In a humorous way, Luke recounts how Peter was left standing at the gate of the courtyard while the disciples refused to believe that he could possibly be there!

12:15 It's his angel. It was believed that each person had a guardian angel who watched over that individual. Assuming that Peter was killed, the only solution the disciples could come up with was that Peter's angel had taken on Peter's form.

12:17 James. This is the brother of Jesus (Mark 6:3). James did not believe in Jesus as the Messiah during Jesus' ministry (John 7:5), but after the resurrection, Jesus appeared to him in a special way (1 Cor. 15:7) qualifying James to be an apostle. James became a leader in the Jerusalem church (15:13; 21:18; Gal. 2:9) and his piety and devotion to God gained the respect of the Jewish community in general. When executed by the Sadducean high priest in A.D. 61 his death was mourned by many Pharisaic

Jews as well as Christians. **he departed and went to a different place**. While Peter recognized his release as an act of God, he did not believe that made him invulnerable to Herod's plots. Thus, he left Jerusalem for some time. Although Peter was in Jerusalem at the time of the council in Acts 15, nothing more is told of his story in Acts. Church tradition associates him with travels to Alexandria, Asia Minor, and finally Rome where he was crucified upside down by the Emperor Nero.

SESSION 8

MISSION & MULTIPLICATION

SCRIPTURE: ACTS 8:1-8,14-17

Last week we looked at the importance of prayer, both in the early church and in group life. This week, in our final session, we will see how the early church spread after it was dispersed from one central church in Jerusalem. We will use this story as a springboard to talk about the mission of our small groups and our need to multiply in order to strengthen the church.

If anything in the natural world is truly alive, it will grow, and that is a pretty good test for groups as well. Groups that are alive are like biological cells. They grow and divide, divide and grow. That is why we do not encourage groups that simply maintain and never change. We encourage groups that divide an give birth to other groups. Each healthy small group will move through various stages as it matures.

• **Birth Stage**: This is the time in which group members form relationships and begin to develop community. The group will spend more time in icebreaker exercises, relational Bible study, and covenant building.

• **Growth Stage**: Here the group begins to care for one another as it learns to apply what they learn through Bible study, to worship together, and hold up one another in prayer.

• **Develop Stage**: Inductive Bible study deepens while the group members discover and develop gifts and skills. The group explores ways to invite their neighbors and coworkers to group meetings. New leadership is developed as the group moves toward multiplication into new groups.

• **Multiply Stage**: The group begins the multiplication process. Members pray about their involvement in new groups. The "new" groups begin the life cycle again with the Birth Stage.

Ten Steps for Multiplying Small Groups

1. **Share a vision**: From the very first meeting of a group the vision must be cast for the mission. God can greatly affect the larger body of Christ through a small group if there is a vision for creating new groups and bringing people into the kingdom. If the group will make a group covenant that envisions multiplying into new groups, then new groups will happen. An effective leader will regularly keep this goal in front of the group. It is essential to raise up group leaders from your

group and to divide into new groups every 18–24 months. Announce the intention to multiply early and often.

2. **Build a new leadership team**: As the group matures through the Growth and Develop Stages, the present leadership team should identify apprentice leaders and facilitators. This is done best in a small-group setting. Look for an engineer type as the group administrator, the party animal as the hospitality person, a person that loves interaction and knowledge as the facilitator, and a caring person to handle group shepherding. Next you must seek to train and mentor them as they grow in confidence. Here is an outline of this process:
   a. Identify apprentice leaders and facilitators
   b. Provide on-the-job training
   c. Give them the opportunity to lead your group
   d. Introduce the new team to your church
   e. Launch the new group

3. **Determine the type of group**: Who are you trying to reach? There are four commonly identified audiences: a "core" audience consists of those in your congregation who are the leaders and the heart of the congregation; the "congregation" consist of those who are basically the regular participants who can be counted on to be present at most events; the "crowd" includes members and other participants that come to worship at least occasionally; and "seekers" are those who have not been church-attenders in the past, but who are now spiritually seeking.

	Group	Percentage	Group Type
a.	Core	10%	Discipleship Group
b.	Congregation	30%	Pulpit or Care Groups
c.	Crowd	60%	Felt Need Groups
d.	Seekers	Outsiders	Support Groups
e.		All	Affinity Groups
f.		All	Covenant Groups

4. **Conduct a Felt Need Survey**: Use either a custom survey for your church or the one included in this book to determine an area or a specific topic for your first study.

5. **Choose curriculum**: Make sure your choice fits the group type and the stage in the life cycle of your group. All Serendipity courses are pre-selected for stage of the life cycle.

6. **Ask someone to serve as host**: Determine when and where the group will meet. Someone must coordinate the following.
   a. Where the meeting will be held.
   b. Who will provide babysitters (if necessary).
   c. Who will teach children (if necessary).
   d. Who will provide refreshments.

7. **Find out who will go with the new team**: There are several options in beginning new groups.
   a. Encourage several members of your group to go with the new leadership team to start a new group.
   b. The existing leadership team will leave to start a new group leaving the existing group with the new team.
   c. Several groups can break off beginning all new groups.

8. **Begin countdown**: Use a study designed to help multiply groups, building each week until you launch your new group.

9. **Celebrate**: Have a party with presents for the new group. Make announcements to your church, advertising the new group and its leadership team.

10. **Keep casting a vision**: Remember as you start new groups to keep casting a vision for multiplying into new groups.

 ICEBREAKER   *Connect with your Group* | **15 Min.**

***LEADER**

Assign a member of the group to lead this Icebreaker. If there is someone in the group who has not done so yet, he or she should be chosen. In leading the Icebreaker it is important to have each person share. Take turns answering two or three of the Icebreaker questions.

The church suffered hardship right from the beginning. But, out of difficult situations God built a strong vibrant organism. He provided the Holy Spirit to bring this young body of believers through great oppression. What has been your experience with this? Share your own experience with feeling like you were in a hard place and you were forced to grow.

1. What is the hardest move you have had to make in your life? What do you remember as being especially hard to leave behind when you made this move?

2. In the move you spoke about, what "serendipity" (unexpected delightful surprise) did you find in the place to which you moved?

3. In terms of the Old West, are you more of a "pioneer-explorer" (one who likes to go new places and try new things), or a "settler" (one who likes to out down roots and stay where you are)?

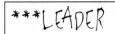

We generally think of persecution as something negative with a destructive effect. However, in the early history of the church there were some positive effects of the persecution they went through. For one thing, it strengthened the faith of many by allowing them to identify with the suffering of their Lord and Savior Jesus Christ. However, it also helped direct- ly with the spread of the faith. The natural tendency of the first believers was to stay in their own city. Thus, since most people came to faith in Jerusalem, that is where they lived and wanted to stay. How- ever, persecution in Jerusalem drove them out of that city (and out of their "comfort zone"), and forced them to other parts of the world, where they shared their faith and helped the church spread. This reminds us that as comfortable as it may be to stay in one place and one group forever, the mission of the kingdom to reach others requires us to move out and multiply. As you read the story, think of your own feel- ings about staying in a comfortable place, and God's call for you to move on.

8 ... On that day a severe persecution broke out against the church in Jerusalem, and all except the apostles were scattered throughout the land of Judea and Samaria. [2] But devout men buried Stephen and mourned deeply over him. [3] Saul, however, was ravaging the church, and he would enter house after house, drag off men and women, and put them in prison.

[4] So those who were scattered went on their way proclaiming the message of good news. [5] Philip went down to a city in Samaria and preached the Messiah to them. [6] The crowds paid attention with one mind to what Philip said, as they heard and saw the signs he was performing. [7] For unclean spirits, crying out with a loud voice, came out of many who were possessed, and many who were paralyzed and lame were healed. [8] So there was great joy in that city.

... [14] When the apostles who were at Jerusalem heard that Samaria had welcomed God's message, they sent Peter and John to them. [15] After they went down there, they prayed for them, that they might receive the Holy Spirit. [16] For He had not yet come down on any of them; they had only been baptized in the name of the Lord Jesus. [17] Then Peter and John laid their hands on them, and they received the Holy Spirit.

Acts 8:1-8,14-17

QUESTIONS FOR INTERACTION

***LEADER

Divide the group into subgroups of three to six persons each, and assign someone to lead each subgroup. It is best to assign people who did not have the chance to lead in recent weeks.

Refer to the Summary and Study Notes at the end of this section as needed. If 30 minutes is not enough time to answer all of the questions in this section, conclude the Bible Study by answering questions 7 and 8.

1. When you were a child or teen, where do you remember being driven out of?
   · The living room during my parents' parties
   · A sibling's bedroom.
   · The parties I crashed.
   · R-rated movies when I tried to sneak in.
   · The nice restaurants when I embarrassed my parents.
   · A neighbor's yard or garden when I went in looking for my ball.
   · other _____

2. Were you one of the disciples driven out of Jerusalem during this time, how would you have felt about this big change?

3. What is the significance of the fact that many of the disciples were scattered into Samaria (see Notes vv. 1b-3,5)?

4. How did the disciples respond to being "scattered" (v. 4)?

5. How did the Samaritans respond to Phillip's message? What did he do that especially made them pay attention to what he said?

6. Why were Peter and John sent to Samaria? What did they want to make sure happened? Why was this so important?

7. How are you feeling right now about this group being "scattered" to start new groups? What is hard about this process? Why is it important?

8. What has happened in this group that you want to make sure also happens in the group you lead?

GOING DEEPER: *If your group has time and/or wants a challenge, go on to this question.*

9. While the disciples were scattered throughout Judea and Samaria, they still remained connected with each other through the apostles. In what ways will the people in this group remain connected to each other? How can that connection be nurtured?

10. What role does the Holy Spirit play in developing a successful group (vv. 14-17)? What should a leader do to include the Spirit in the group?

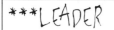 **CARING TIME** *Apply the Lesson & Pray for One another* | **15 Min.**

***LEADER

Bring the group back together and begin the Caring Time by sharing responses to the first two questions. Then encourage group members to pray at will in relation to the concerns and praises that have been shared, before you close. Then proceed to the commissioning described in question 3.

1. What has happened in this group that are you most thankful for?

2. How can this group continue to pray for the challenges you will face as a small-group leader?

3. One at a time, have each group member go to the center of the circle and kneel. Then have the rest of the group gather around the person, and place their hands on him or her. Pray for the Holy Spirit to empower that person and commission them to the new group they will lead. Make sure everyone is included and that every person in the group has the opportunity to pray for one other person in the group.

 NOTES ON ACTS 8:1-8,14-17

Summary: The apostles have remained in Jerusalem in spite of widespread persecution. It is probably aimed at the Greek-speaking converts who shared Stephen's view of the temple. The persecution throughout Judea and Samaria forces the spread of the gospel out from Jerusalem. With the movement out of the message the church leaders have no choice but to respond to the work of God, and Peter and John find themselves being instruments of the Holy Spirit coming upon the believers from Samaria.

8:1b-3 The church's spread to Judea and Samaria shows that God used even this persecution to demonstrate afresh that he is not limited to Jerusalem (1:8)! In a sense this persecution was like blowing on dandelion seeds — what looks like an act of destruction is simply spreading the seed.

8:3 Saul, however... Whether 26:10 is sufficient evidence that Saul belonged to the Sanhedrin is uncertain, but he quickly became the leading figure in a violent persecution of the church. **was ravaging**. This word is used to describe how a beast rips the flesh off its victim. Saul's persecution led to other Christians being condemned to death as well (9:1-2).

8:5 Samaria. When the northern kingdom of Israel was conquered by the Assyrians (722 B.C.), many of its people were deported while exiles from elsewhere in the vast Assyrian empire were brought in (2 Kings 17:23-41). These people intermarried with the remaining Israelites and adopted some of their religious practices. As a result, the Jews of the southern kingdom considered the Samaritans as religious compromisers and racial half-breeds. By Jesus' day, strict Jews avoided Samaria and "Samaritan" was used as an insult (John 8:48). As a Greek-speaking Jew, Philip may have been less prejudiced against the Samaritans than the Palestinian Jews allowing him to speak freely with them.

8:6-8 Philip's ministry was like that of the apostles' ministries in that he too was empowered by the Spirit to perform signs and wonders that confirmed his message.

8:8 great joy. Joy is the characteristic emotion Luke ascribes to people when they place their faith in Jesus (Luke 24:52).

8:14-17 Upon hearing that widespread faith in Jesus had broken out in Samaria, the apostles apparently decided they needed to check out the situation (11:22-23). Thus, Peter and John are sent as representatives to investigate. While there are various interpretations for the delay between the Samaritans' response of faith and their reception of the Spirit, the one that best fits the context of Acts is that it occurred so that the apostles could be convinced that God was indeed including the Samaritans as full members of his church (1:8; 10:44-45; 11:15). While water baptism and the reception of the Spirit are clearly linked in Acts, there is no fixed chronological formula for the connection. Luke's theological emphasis implies that each situation is governed by his desire to show that all types of people are to be included in God's church rather than by any other theological consideration.

8:16 baptized in the name of the Lord Jesus. Their baptism affirmed a commitment to live in loyalty to Jesus as the Messiah. That there were baptized Christians who had yet to receive the power of the Holy Spirit is also pointed out in Acts 19:1-7.

PERSONAL NOTES

PERSONAL NOTES